LETTERS TO MY SON
ON THE LOVE OF
BOOKS

Also by Roberto Cotroneo

Presto con Fuoco

Otranto

LETTERS TO MY SON ON THE LOVE OF BOOKS

Roberto Cotroneo *1961-*

Translated from the Italian by N. S. Thompson

THE ECCO PRESS

THE ECCO PRESS
100 West Broad Street
Hopewell, New Jersey 08525

Published simultaneously in Canada by Penguin Books Canada Ltd., Ontario
Printed in the United States of America

Library of Congress Cataloging-in-Publication Data
Cotroneo, Roberto, 1961–
[Se una mattina d'estate un bambino. English]
Letters to my son on the love of books / Roberto Cotroneo;
translated from the Italian by N. S. Thompson. — 1st ed.
p.   cm.
Includes bibliographical references (p. 153).
ISBN 0-88001-631-0
1. American Literature —20th century—History and criticism.
2. Stevenson, Robert Louis, 1850–1894. Treasure island.
3. Salinger, J. D. (Jerome David), 1919– Catcher in the rye.
4. Eliot, T. S. (Thomas Stearns), 1888–1965—Criticism and interpretation.
5. Books and reading.   I. Title.
PS221.C6413 1998
810.9'005—dc21
98-7773
CIP

Designed by Typeworks
The text of this book is set in ACaslon
9 8 7 6 5 4 3 2 1
FIRST EDITION 1998

To Federica,

who knows how to tell you

the most beautiful stories . . .

LETTERS TO MY SON
ON THE LOVE OF
BOOKS

ONCE UPON A TIME, THERE WAS A LADYBUG . . .

Dear Francesco,

You came in this morning and brought me your book. You were still full of sleep, your small dark eyes were struggling to open, and you were walking awkwardly with one foot in front of the other so that it looked as if you might collapse at any moment. You came in carrying your picture book—the spiral-bound one about a ladybug—which you love so much and which your mother reads to you before you go to sleep. We bought it for you because one day in the park I put a ladybug on the back of your hand for you to see. It ran up toward your wrist and you watched it with that mixture of curiosity and comprehension that children like you have. You waited to see what the creature would do so that you could capture it and keep it, but just at that very moment it flew away and left you disappointed. You never imagined that would happen. A ladybug doesn't look as if it can fly. When you first see one, it looks as if it's an entirely earthbound creature. Then, when we were home, you suddenly asked your mother to tell you a story about a ladybug. Or rather, what I should say is that you didn't make an articulate request like that, because—even though you're learning to recognize many words—you still can't speak, but you said something like "Ladybug story" (or more precisely still "'adybug 'tory," which is your way of saying it). So we told you that once upon a time there was a ladybug who lived in the park and one day a boy called Francesco caught it in his hand. It was a red ladybug with white spots and was happy to crawl about on Francesco's hand. Then a yellow ladybug friend with blue spots called to it from far away and said, "Come on, let's fly away to a beautiful place!" And so the red ladybug flew away with the yellow ladybug to a place that was full of adventures.

Did you realize that this was one of your very first stories, Francesco? Perhaps it might be more correct to say that you felt that you really needed a story. A few days later, we bought you that little book, the spiral-bound one with the large red ladybug on the cover, so that you could remember how it looked. That picture book then became a story, which was always different each time. It's strange: books have always been familiar, even everyday, things for you; our house is full of them, thousands and thousands of them, and I've never forbidden you to touch them; on the contrary, I've always said you could handle them, but never to tear the pages. In the same way, I've never stopped you touching the piano; you can play it when you want, and sit there, as tiny as you are, at the huge grand piano and thump away at the keys, even if you do sometimes make a terrible din. And to think that at first you even asked for music on the stand, so that you could play like your father who often sight reads the music.

Now we come to it, this business of reading. You've always seen us reading books and newspapers or writing on those evenings when you wish to stay up—which is almost always— and ask to see *Peter Pan* or *The Jungle Book* one more time. And many a time you've asked us to read to you the books which are now beginning to take their place on the shelves, such as *Dumbo* and *Cinderella,* those that play music when you touch the picture or those which open and become a merry-go-round or a little theater, or those in the shape of one of your animals, the ones you've come to recognize and give a name to. So all rabbits, like the one which lives in a hutch on the terrace, are called Lulu; and all crocodiles are called Crock, like the one who wants to devour Captain Hook and which you can hear when it gets near because of the ticking of the alarm clock it swallowed long ago.

Dear Francesco, on this morning of summer and seaside you woke me up and asked me, "Dad, story," bringing me your ladybug book. Your hair was still ruffled, your blond curls just a mite tangled, and you had nothing on your feet. I told you to sit down on the step and I began to think that this book could start right here, with your aware and attentive, and often very serious, face; with your *s*'s pronounced like *t*'s which make you sound like a cartoon. For the time being, the story of a ladybug or Dumbo is enough to satisfy you. Later, you'll change and want to read other things, not books with pictures of animals or those which play tunes. You'll hear of something called literature, and also poetry; you'll learn nursery rhymes by heart and perhaps even forget the ending, and everyone will be amused. Also, while you're young, you'll run the risk of some kindhearted teacher trying to instill in you the almost sacred value of study—the need to read and acquire knowledge—but who makes you feel like a minute insect facing the vast mountain ranges of universal genius, and won't show you how to climb up, but only to stand and photograph them like any old tourist. As I suffer from vertigo, I have no desire to make you into a literary mountaineer, Francesco, but I do want you to understand that admiration should always be the end result of a process, and never its beginning, otherwise it's only like an illusion, or like falling in love, and therefore something completely different.

Dear Francesco, it's my job to be a critic, in particular a literary critic. I'm paid to express my opinion on the books I read. And for the moment, I'm paid to express my opinion on books I don't like. It is an exercise in style and, after all, it's easier to find poor books rather than good ones. My work also serves those readers who don't want to make a mistake, who don't frequent bookshops and need someone with greater expertise than theirs. I've always explained to you that books should be treated well, that you should leaf through them carefully so as not to tear the pages. But I've also said that books aren't sacred; they shouldn't be kept whatever the cost. The worth of a book doesn't lie in the fact that one day someone bound together a number of pages full of words. You should treasure the good books, and throw away the ones which are not good. In this house, the books which surround you are mostly good ones, precisely because many others have not found a place here, ending up elsewhere or in the waste-paper basket. Don't be afraid, dear Francesco; in time you won't become like many people who, because they stand in awe of culture, are afraid to have anything to do with it, joke about it, be paradoxical about it, or even enter into dialogue with authors without putting themselves a good many rungs lower on the ladder. You shouldn't be afraid of literature, Francesco, not even the most difficult. You should never say: you mean you've read Joyce, all of him, every page? You should joke with Joyce, he would have appreciated it. And don't turn the most disturbing and complex poetry into a monad, into something to be admired for its useless grandeur. Dante's poetry should be learned by heart, as if it were a nursery rhyme, except the rhythm is given by the tercets, and not the guitar of Bob Marley, whom you already ask to hear.

I won't turn you into a presumptuous person (although a little presumption is a good self-defense); instead I want to accompany you through a much more difficult operation which has always had a limited chance of success: that of counteracting a good part of the commonplaces that too many people will try to put into your head. I can just picture you with your dark, very lively eyes. You won't easily think well of many things, or be convinced of that which isn't always true. You're not the kind of child to whom one can simply say that is how it is, believe me. You have an ironic and transgressive nature, as many will come to find. Sometimes it will be the turn of your mother and me, and that won't be easy, but that's all right.

Can one write a letter in the form of a book to explain to you the pleasure of reading? The answer lies in the existence of this book, which is a slightly different way of telling you the story of the ladybug. In the end, there's not a great deal of difference between that story and those I'm going to tell you about here. Dumbo is finally able to fly, and has the last laugh on the circus. Roger earns a great deal of money at the expense of Cruella De Vil and is able to start breeding Dalmatians. And Captain Hook is endlessly pursued by the crocodile that has never forgotten the excellent flavor of his hand. Those stories will weave into others and you'll come to substitute Stephen Dedalus perhaps for Peter Pan; although it's much more likely that you'll let them coexist in the play of your memory which will sometimes come to amaze you. Don't be surprised that the more you confuse things, the more you mix authors up, the more the titles and the centuries become mingled in your mind, the more you'll have understood something about literature. If it happens that the latest and most stupid hit record brings to your mind a fragment of Heraclitus, then it will mean that, on the cultural side, you have nothing to worry about at all.

In high school, I had a teacher who didn't teach me a great deal of English, but he did teach me about literature without putting it on a higher pedestal or worshipping it. He simply came into our class of fifteen-year-olds and asked, "Have you ever heard of Dr. Johnson?" He meant Samuel Johnson, but specifically James Boswell's *Life of Samuel Johnson,* a biography well over a thousand pages long. Not one of us had ever heard of it, but it was his particular genius to get us kids to read books like that without forcing us to. I owe it to him for introducing me to some of the most important books I have ever read, but more importantly, he taught me an invaluable method. I can still recall his thick-rimmed glasses, his still-not-white hair, and his habitual gray suit. And, as people did then, he also smoked. He would come into the classroom with an ironic expression and ask, "Do you know Joyce? No? Then you're ignorant!" But he said it in a joking manner, not as an insult. He used the word "ignorant" in its true etymological sense: "unaware." We were unaware of the existence of James Joyce, Laurence Sterne, or Virginia Woolf. It helped us to be called ignorant by a man who knew what the maieutic system was in philosophy. At the age of fifteen I was reading Joyce, T. S. Eliot's *The Waste Land,* and much more. It was my introduction to an intellectual education. I can remember the emotion when I discovered the pleasure of discussing the "objective correlative," what Joyce's meaning of epiphany was, and the way the narrative tenses flow together in Virginia Woolf's *To the Lighthouse*. It was all invaluable. At the right age of adolescence, I was able to give vent to the desire for interpretation, especially the most way out, which often elicits—in people who basically don't like books—irony. Every so often somebody asks me if you can learn to write clearly. My answer is that simplicity demands a constant intellectual effort, a gymnastics of the mind.

"Have you ever heard of Dr. Johnson?" my ancient teacher of English used to ask back in the Seventies. I use the word "ancient" as it is used in the poem *The Rime of the Ancient Mariner*. That is a poem, Francesco, by the English Romantic poet Samuel Taylor Coleridge. It has often been translated into Italian as "The Ballad of the Old Sailor," but that's a mistake. Coleridge's sailor is timeless, as ancient and yet as near as the cliffs rising vertically from the sea. "Old" is something less defined: an old sailor is someone still living in the present, who can still change and is subject to change. It's therefore inaccurate to translate the "ancient mariner" as the "old sailor." You'll come to see, Francesco, that poetry is an interlocking puzzle, where even titles have to be interpreted with precision. I will speak more of this later, when I talk about T. S. Eliot.

But I was telling you about my teacher and Dr. Johnson. True, it was all a long time ago, and I don't know if I can credit him with even the little I do know about literature, or if I'm adding something in the way of interest on the capital he laid down. It doesn't really matter. What I hope is that you encounter a teacher like him, who—before anything else—knows how to *teach*; a teacher who knows how to communicate, no matter what the subject. He was—and is (although he no longer teaches)—one of the few true intellectuals I ever met. And I might say that my work has allowed me to mingle with many of Italy's most accomplished minds. Although he may no longer be one today, he was a Communist, albeit an unorthodox one. He was a libertarian, but with strange blind spots borne of the Cold War. One day I didn't take part in a student protest and came to class. He was sitting at his desk and looked at me in amazement. He asked me why I had come to class. I replied that I didn't agree with the protest, and he rejoined peremptorily, "Remember what Lenin said: it's better to be wrong inside the Party, than be correct outside it." It is a dictum that I wouldn't agree with even under torture, but it belongs to a world which, today, because it is gone, I miss. It was a world of intellectual rigor, where a man like him invited us to read Chomsky's *Syntactic Structures* and addressed us children—who had only just left puberty—as if we were adults.

Today, dear Francesco, I miss people like that teacher, people who were capable of ranging from one subject to another with a remarkable level of intelligence. I hope you will have the same good fortune that I had because only people like that can help you understand the dream that this book is about: that literature isn't simply a game of the intellect, but a way of understanding the world. It is the only way one can put on the lenses of ambiguity, which nobody today, it seems, wears anymore.

Don't be taken in by what people say, Francesco; they will try to tell you that life is more complex than literature. It's not true. The literary world of Marcel Proust is infinitely more complex than the real one. Leopold Bloom's day is completely different from that of an ordinary Dubliner, even the most refined. Literature is a world of analogy, where books can speak to each other. To enter that world, you have to make a leap beyond this world. And afterward, the return is difficult because the characters you meet will continue to speak to you, to advise you, and to influence your decisions. One of the important films of my adolescence was Woody Allen's *Play It Again, Sam,* where the main character is always talking to the figure of Rick from the film *Casablanca.* He's very unsure of himself with women, but knows that Rick will tell him what to do. It is a play of cinematic quotation, a comic method of making the awkward timidity of the main character even more evident. However, it is true that life and literature interweave in such a marked, but differentiated, way.

Besides, you are already experimenting like that yourself now and have been doing so since before you were two years old. You would take something from *The Jungle Book,* your favorite character Colonel Hathi, and transform him into something concrete, something that really existed. He became the elephant in Rome's zoo who (although you shouldn't) you throw peanuts to. For you, he's Hathi. By the same process, the tiger in the nearby cage is Shere Khan. They derive from a book and film animation, find themselves in the zoo, and then return to the book and the film animation. There is no distinction, the parallel worlds interweave, then separate. What reader of Joyce hasn't thought, even fleetingly, while visiting Dublin that he has seen somebody with the face of Stephen Dedalus? And on a sleepless night, what child hasn't imagined seeing Peter Pan's ship sailing through the sky? I want to teach you to see that ship; I want to write a book to tell you that serious books, even those difficult ones for adults, are nothing more than sailing ships in disguise and have the same magic as the ship sprinkled with gold dust sailed by Peter Pan. And do you know something, Francesco? Learn to put your faith in a person who loves to read, in a person who always carries a book of poetry with them; and likewise be suspicious of anyone who tells you that literature's a good thing, but they've no time for it, that you can read when you're young, but later . . . They're lying and they know it. It doesn't mean a thing to them.

But let's leave this topic, Francesco, and return to the ship on which Tinker Bell sprinkled gold dust. This is another of the stories you like to hear. You always want to hear about the pirates, about Tiger Lily, about Michael and Wendy and the dog called Nana who acts as babysitter. Often you have very precise ideas about the stories you want to be told. Sometimes it's Dumbo, sometimes it's Roger in *101 Dalmatians,* and other times it's the boy cub in *The Jungle Book,* but more and more you want your stories mixed together, so that

Dumbo and his mother Jumbo mingle with Hathi and Pongo and the Siamese cats in *Lady and the Tramp*. You're beginning to create a very simple process, that of making books speak to each other. One day, Francesco, you'll come to learn that this is what the great critics do. They put different books in touch with each other in order to discover more about the world. They search for continual clues to establish relationships which perhaps had never been perceived before. What would happen if Captain Hook met Long John Silver? Or Black Dog, who was the more fortunate because he was able to keep two fingers on one of his hands, while Captain Hook gave the whole of one of his hands to the crocodile. I'll tell you about these characters, Francesco, and about much more.

However, I will not tell you too much, because this book is made from only a few books, but they were chosen with great care so as to give you an idea of literature different from the one I suspect you'll be given at school. First of all, I'll tell you about *Treasure Island* by Robert Louis Stevenson, which is perhaps his most famous book. Everybody thinks it is simply a children's book , which it is, but not in the sense that most people think. It is one not because it is simple, or obvious, or because it tells of an adventure about pirates, battles, and boardings, and has you holding your breath. No, Francesco, *Treasure Island* is a children's book because it *teaches* one how subtle and ambiguous the line between good and evil is; and also how adventure is a painful pathway in life, but one that can't be avoided.

After that, I'll tell you about another author, one still living today. He's a strange man named J. D. Salinger who wrote *The Catcher in the Rye*. I'll tell you about this book in order to explain to you not only what transgression is, but also tenderness, and how both transgression and tenderness can be fellow travelers (and basically, you're a tender transgressor).

After we understand what it means to be tender and transgressive, we will leave the world of childhood and adolescence to enter the world of poetry. We will read two poems together, or to be precise, a poem and a sequence of poems by another author in the English language, T. S. Eliot. The poem is called "The Love Song of J. Alfred Prufrock" and the sequence is "The Waste Land." You will come to know why the women in the rooms come and go, talking of Michelangelo and why Madame Sosostris, famous clairvoyant, is the wisest woman in Europe. You will come to understand how the protagonist of the poem feels he is losing something important, how he cannot even speak anymore, and how great events can seem so small and how small things can disturb the universe ("Do I dare disturb the universe?" he asks).

The final author I will tell you about is perhaps the most complex. By using him I will try to explain what are some of the most difficult things of all to understand: the possession of innate talent, which some people have and others do not; the effort of comparing oneself with others; and the struggle to escape mediocrity without ever losing sight of humility. I also want to explain what genius is, and envy and, above all, what great music is. The author this time is Thomas Bernhard, an Austrian, and the book is a novel called *The Loser*.

You'll also hear about Glenn Gould, the great Canadian pianist, whom you've heard since you were very small ("Daddy, Bach" you say when you want to hear his *Italian Concerto*), and about how talent can become an obsession.

I won't give you any idea of the ending, Francesco, but will only say that it will be a tale, a fable. I will tell you about a venerable old man, a castle, and about many characters who sit down to listen to an extraordinary lesson about literature, the world and the world of literature. Naturally, there will be no summing up, because that doesn't exist in the world of literature where nothing comes to an end. Everything remains ambiguous, fluid. A book is never static. Sometimes, for this reason, re-reading a book is even more stimulating than discovering it the first time. But you will soon come to learn this. In the meantime, let's try to remember . . . how does the story about the ladybug begin? As you know, Francesco, the beginning is always different. And this time it begins like this: "I remember him as if it were yesterday, as he came plodding to the inn door, his sea-chest following behind him in a handbarrow; a tall, strong, heavy, nut-brown man; his tarry pigtail falling over the shoulders of his soiled blue coat . . ."

ANXIETY

Sometimes you feel afraid, Francesco, although it's not that you are a fearful child. Sometimes you ask me to go along with you. You take my hand and, a little worried, you say "Come on, Daddy." You don't like going into a dark room and, on occasion, you like being accompanied to the end of the hall. I try to explain to you that you shouldn't be afraid, and invite you to show some courage, but I don't force you because a little fear is good for you; it helps you, makes you stronger when you're an adult, especially if your fears are reasonable ones and you learn both to overcome and respect them. But I also realize that when you take my hand and lead me down the hall, that you want me to accompany you to a place of adventure, somewhere faraway. You want to see what will happen. You're still so young that the distant island where anything can happen is either the kitchen or the dark study. But in that kitchen and in that study, there is a world you have to come to grips with, because that is where you will find pirates and unexpected traps. It is in the far-off places that one comes to grips with life. It is not by chance that Jim

Hawkins begins his tale with the words, "I remember him as if it were yesterday." The things that strike you most remain clear in the mind, losing none of their color. They remain there, fixed, like the best of your memories or the worst of your nightmares.

Treasure Island is the story of a nightmare, painted in garish colors; an adventure that is exotic, but still a nightmare. People will tell you it is a book for children. At home, we have many editions of it, some of them with illustrations, and even an old edition your mother found on a bookstall in Bologna that she gave me as a present with a very loving dedication. As you look through them, you will, at first, be convinced that it is a story about pirates. You will then begin to feel a slight anxiety, the same one that grips a reader when they begin *The Turn of the Screw* by Henry James, except that Stevenson is not as explicit—you have to be well practiced at reading between the lines. In James's novella the two children come to a terrible fate, and you know that it will end in disaster. In *Treasure Island* everything sails along with the wind astern and the seemingly wicked characters, the dreadful looking ones, disappear from the early chapters, deceiving everyone. You see, Francesco, when I read the book for the first time as a child I was afraid of the wrong people. My nightmare was meeting Blind Pew. You will be frightened when you come to the chapter called "The Black Spot." Jim is a likeable boy who has lived a normal life without any great problems until, one day, a knock on the door brings the captain with his tarred pigtail, his sea-chest, his clasp-knife, and his frightening song:

"Fifteen men on the dead man's chest—
  Yo-ho-ho, and a bottle of rum!
Drink and the devil had done for the rest—
  Yo-ho-ho, and a bottle of rum!"

It's not a pleasant song, is it, Francesco? But pirates, real pirates, don't play around. They're cruel, so cruel as to appear stupid. They're also weak and greedy, and among the worst people you could ever possibly meet. Jim must have become aware of this when he first met the man with "his hands ragged and scarred, with black, broken nails; and the sabre cut across one cheek, a dirty, livid white." This is the old sea dog, Bill, or—as he calls himself—the "Captain." Bill is a vagabond who sailed with Flint, the most feared pirate on the high seas, and he owns a very important map that shows the position of Flint's treasure. Apart from the other pirates, no one knows of its existence, let alone Jim and his parents, who run the little inn called "The Admiral Benbow." The Captain's presence disturbs the everyday life of this English family living at the beginning of the eighteenth century: he drinks too much, doesn't pay his bills, and has a violent nature. It is in these early pages, Francesco, that the lines are made unclear. The terrible Bill announces himself in all his loud and conceited banality, but he is simply a joke of a pirate or—to be more precise—he is made to appear so. One evening when he tries to go too far, the rum having made more than its usual mark, he is first threatened, then silenced by Dr. Livesey. Billy Bones is nothing more than Stevenson's

means to force Jim on a journey that will take him from adolescence, with its inevitable pain and damage, into adulthood.
With Billy's arrival, Jim's father falls ill, then after some time,
dies, and everything at the inn becomes more difficult. Jim
and his mother find it an increasing effort to look after so
troublesome a guest as the captain, especially when he starts
to receive visits from Black Dog and Blind Pew.

Some pages back I spoke to you about good and evil and
about why this novel is a kind of journey of initiation into life.
It is a complex journey where many characters come into
play: main characters who appear minor, and vice versa. It is a
novel that has none of the linearity or apparent simplicity of
certain oriental tales of initiation. When you are grown up,
you will read books like René Daumal's *Mount Analogue*[1] and
understand that there are many ways of overcoming the obstacles that life places in your path: sometimes they are linear,
with progressive steps; but they can also take a different course
and follow a more shifting, circuitous path, where it seems
that you slide about, taking two steps forward and one step
back. Books are also like that, Francesco, they digress and
speak of other things, before returning to the main subject
with an added something. *Treasure Island* is a novel about a
journey that is very different from what it first announces itself to be. It is about the end of innocence: it is true that it is
a book for children, but once they read it, and read it carefully
(although perhaps a single reading won't suffice), then they
can only grow.

As a child, I was frightened of Blind Pew, not Long John

Silver or the Captain. I was afraid of Pew and Black Dog. Stevenson excels at mixing up his characters for us and, above all, for Jim Hawkins. Here is what the boy says: "about three o'clock of a bitter, foggy, frosty afternoon, I was standing at the door for a moment . . . when I saw someone drawing slowly near along the road. He was plainly blind, for he tapped before him with a stick, and wore a great green shade over his eyes and nose; and he was hunched, as if with age or weakness, and wore a huge old tattered sea-cloak with a hood, that made him appear positively deformed. I never saw in my life a more dreadful-looking figure."

I never saw in my life a more dreadful-looking figure. The narration has shades and ambiguous contours. The cold is bitter and it's foggy. The scene is blurred. Jim is standing on the threshold of the inn. Pew asks him for help, pretending not to know where he is. The boy replies, "You are at the 'Admiral Benbow,'" and Pew says softly, "I hear a voice . . . a young voice. Will you give me your hand, my kind young friend, and lead me in?" The suspense is drawn out. The beggar is dreadful-looking, as we already know. We also know that somebody is looking for the Captain, but we don't know that there is a treasure map at stake. Pew is there, however, to show the stupidity of evil and the havoc caused by wickedness. Stevenson leaves you holding your breath and goes on: "I held out my hand, and the horrible, soft-spoken, eyeless creature gripped it in a moment like a vice. I was so much startled that I struggled to withdraw; but the blind man pulled me close up to him with a single action of his arm./

'Now, boy,' he said, 'take me in to the captain.'" Everything proceeds rapidly from the slow tapping of the stick, to the "soft-spoken" voice and the young one in counterpoint to it, then there is a change of register. Jim is suddenly startled by the vice-like grip. It will frighten you, Francesco, as it frightened me. Then it becomes worse, because at Jim's refusal ("Sir . . . upon my word I dare not"), Pew becomes terrifying and responds: "'Oh,' he sneered, 'that's it! Take me in straight, or I'll break your arm.'/ And he gave it, as he spoke, a wrench that made me cry out./'Sir,' I said, 'it is for yourself I mean. The captain is not what he used to be. He sits with a drawn cutlass. Another gentleman—'/ 'Come, now, march,' interrupted he; and I never heard a voice so cruel and cold, and ugly as that blind man's."

Let's pause a moment here, Francesco. Pew is a terrifying pirate who lost his sight when taking a ship in a boarding, the very same in which Long John Silver lost a leg. They were sailing with Flint, a name which inspired fear even many years after the pirate's demise. Now Pew and his companions want to get the pirate's gold back and will go to any lengths to get it. Like Black Dog, the pirate with two fingers missing on his left hand, Pew has squandered everything he earned as a pirate and is now living as a beggar. Being a young boy, Jim has never encountered such shady characters as these. They are real pirates, Francesco, and not like Captain Hook. Boarding ships has left them mutilated, with deep scars often going deeper than the soul. Pew delivers the black spot as a kind of warning or ultimatum to the captain who turns pale when he sees it and collapses heavily to the floor, dead. He dies not only from rum, but from fear. From that moment on, the adventure begins. Jim has only one choice if he wishes to grow: he must go to the island of treasure, become acquainted with Long John Silver, learn what duplicity is, and return home again, with the sound of the sea surf in his ears; but first he must rummage through the captain's sea-chest, after shutting the bolt of the inn door. He has to undertake this with a fear that clutches you by the throat in order to understand that the fear of those shady characters was almost unjustified. Jim and his mother are counting out the money that the captain owed them until, "When we were half-way through, I suddenly put my hand upon her arm; for I had heard in the silent, frosty air a sound that brought my heart into my mouth—the tap-tapping of the blind man's stick upon the frozen road. It drew nearer and nearer, while we sat holding our breath. Then it struck sharp on the inn door, and then we could hear the handle being turned, and the bolt rattling as the wretched being tried to enter." In the icy air, Blind Pew has come back, right up to the door, but the bolt keeps him back. Now there is no time left for Jim and his mother. Pew will come back again with the other pirates; he will come back yelling out, ordering them to search everywhere. Jim and his mother escape, but only just in time. Beside himself because Flint's treasure map can no longer be found, Pew cries out: "' —it's that boy. I wish I had put his eyes out!'"

Don't be afraid, Francesco, characters like Pew end up as they should, crushed by the hooves of the horses of the rescuers riding over the countryside. They are stupid people. But Jim doesn't understand. It is too soon for him to be able to take account of something as terrible and as subtle as "cruelty." He is still a child. And yet the captain had warned him: "He had taken me aside one day, and promised me a silver fourpenny on the first of every month if I would only keep my 'weather-eye open for a seafaring man with one leg,'. . . How that personage haunted my dreams, I need scarcely tell you. On stormy nights, when the wind shook the four corners of the house, and the surf roared along the cove and up the cliffs, I would see him in a thousand forms, and with a thousand diabolical expressions. Now the leg would be cut off at the knee, now at the hip; now he was a monstrous kind of a creature who had never had but the one leg, and that in the middle of his body."

The terror of Jim towards a sailor with one leg pales in front of that we call "reality." First it is the "pale, tallowy" Black Dog, then the horrible Pew. When Jim succeeds in showing the map to the Doctor and the Squire they all realize that it is the map of an island on which treasure is buried. A ship is fitted out, good sailors found and—once he is in the port of Bristol—Jim is given the task of locating a certain John Silver. All well and good, but not even at that point do we have any idea of the kind of character Silver is. We have to learn through the ingenuousness of Jim: "Now, to tell you the truth, from the very first mention of Long John . . . I had taken a fear in my mind that he might prove to be the very one-legged sailor whom I had watched for so long at the old

'Benbow.' But one look at the man before me was enough. I had seen the captain, and Black Dog, and the blind man Pew, and I thought I knew what a buccaneer was like—a very different creature, according to me, from this clean and pleasant-tempered landlord."

That's how it is, Francesco, always. The devil always puts on a good face to deceive. A preacher would thunder that evil is more subtle than horror, ghosts, and nightmares that vanish in a night. No, Francesco, you shouldn't believe in these things; you shouldn't be afraid of anyone, nor be distrustful without reason. But if you really are forced (and sometimes you will be, even if I hope you never are), you should beware of men like John Silver. Besides many other things, Stevenson will teach you that. But we will come to it in good time.

We left Jim in Bristol delighting in the sounds and smells of the port, ready to embark on the Hispaniola, the sailing ship that is to take them to the treasure island. We left him unsettled and excited; but before his departure he has time to say goodbye to his mother, even though he still has no idea that departures mean separation, Francesco, where we have to grow by ourselves. Then, with the crew's complement complete, they set sail. By now we know that these sailors are actually pirates who know who has possession of the treasure map. On every page Stevenson leaves us to gather these inferences and, therefore, there is suspense on every page. In fact, the ship's captain intuits something is wrong himself, not being happy about a crew he had no hand in choosing. He therefore asks for a meeting with Dr. Livesey and Squire

Trelawney in order to express his doubts, only to be looked upon as an unbearable troublemaker. At the same time, the two sing the praises of John Silver, whom they consider an honest, trustworthy man. As we know, the opposite is the case. But Stevenson turns around the old saying that appearances are deceptive, here appearances are obvious: the sailors, who have been recruited with such ease, are pirates, and the ship's captain, who is so overly worried about them, is a decent man. But Livesey and Trelawney don't want to listen, being preoccupied with the departure and reaching the island, at whatever the cost. It is not haste with them, but necessity. There is no greed for the treasure, only the need for the task at hand to be completed.

But pay attention here, Francesco. I have guided you through many pages of what the less careful critics merely call an adventure, the expected train of events, even if they are full of intense action. I now want to try to substitute anxiety for fear, and transform the ghosts of childhood into something more adult. Jim Hawkins soon stops being ingenuous. It occurs almost by accident when, by chance, he climbs into an empty barrel of apples, where he eavesdrops on a frightening conversation. We are only a third of the way through the novel and the register changes again: "'No, not I,' said Silver. 'Flint was cap'n; I was quartermaster, along of my timber leg. The same broadside I lost my leg, old Pew lost his deadlights. It was a master surgeon, him that ampytated me—out of college and all—Latin by the bucket, and what not; but he was hanged like a dog, and sun-dried like the rest, at Corso Castle.'"

Thus Long John Silver reveals his true self. He is trying to turn an "honest" sailor to his camp, or rather, he has by now turned him, and as a bonus is indulging in a few memoirs of his past exploits. It is extraordinary how, in a moment, the world of childhood becomes that of the adult. The good-natured Silver exhibits a scorn for everybody, even the surgeon whose Latin and medical degree were not enough to save him being sun-dried at Corso Castle. It is a world where there is not even a thin line between pirates and decent men, simply nothing. Everything can be corrupted and mutiny is drawing ever closer. It is exactly like this in life, Francesco. It is difficult traveling a road that doesn't always have a center line. And with Silver there is no clear dividing line. Listen to what this pirate of many years, who has seen his comrades die of yellow fever, rum, and hardships, says to his youthful admirer about his life and where he sailed: "First with England, then with Flint, that's my story; and now here on my own account, in a manner of speaking. I laid by nine hundred safe, from England, and two thousand after Flint. That ain't bad for a man before the mast—all safe in bank. 'Tain't earning now, it's saving does it, you may lay to that."

But where do they end up, these great pirates like Black Dog? And those English fogs and the terrible threats of Blind Pew? Silenced by horses' hooves. And what about the captain wanting Jim to watch for a "seafaring man with a wooden leg," which became a nightmare for him where he imagined the man as monster with a single leg growing from his middle? Who is this Silver who declares that savings are important, and yet was a pirate with Flint, the most feared buccaneer on the high seas? How many boardings did he see with Flint? How many men did he see hang, how many honest sailors did he kill with his dagger or with his bare hands, and what sneer would have crossed the face of this man whose shipmates called him "Barbecue"? Do you think, Francesco, that the man Billy Bones most feared would be someone who talks about the importance of savings? No, but learning about appearances is one of the lessons of great literature.

There are other lessons: the adult world is cruel and monstrous; by its very nature evil is stupid; criminals and frauds only prosper if they possess a modicum of control; a capacity to simply keep the accounts of life is needed. Silver asks himself: "'Where's all England's men now? I dunno. Where's Flint? Why most on 'em aboard here, and glad to get the duff —been begging before that, some on 'em. Old Pew, as lost his sight, and might have thought shame, spends twelve hundred pounds in a year, like a lord in Parliament. Where is he now? Well, he's dead now and under hatches; but for two year before that, shiver my timbers! The man was starving. He begged, and he stole, and he cut throats, and starved at that.'"

Now do you understand why *Treasure Island* is an important book, Francesco? It teaches you that an adventure is nothing other than a rite of passage. Life's adventures don't help us to discover anything new and they have nothing to do with the fantastic, or with dreams, but help us to grow up, at whatever the cost. For Jim the cost is very great: he comes to know violence, cruelty, betrayal; he has to cope with his own indecisiveness and his feelings of guilt. Finally, and most importantly, he has to live with duplicity and ambiguity. He knows that everything hangs by a thread, but one that is pulled by no one because it is the thread of chance—a fact that many people prefer not to acknowledge. I opened this journey in your company precisely with Stevenson and a book that is very dark and yet appears to be playful and adventurous. When Jim reaches the island there is a deep impression of great happiness; it seems the goal has been reached: "I now felt for the first time the joy of exploration. The isle was uninhabited; my shipmates I had left behind, and nothing lived in front of me but dumb brutes and fowls." But this is really only the beginning. The description of the island is a long and detailed one, but as it proceeds, things gradually become more dramatic: "All at once there began to go a sort of bustle among the bulrushes . . . I judged at once that some of my shipmates must be drawing near along the borders of the fen. Nor was I deceived; for soon I heard the very distant and low tones of a human voice . . . Another voice answered; and then the first voice, which I now recognized to be Silver's . . ." It is indeed Silver who is trying to convince one of the few honest seamen to pass over to his side. He exhorts and threatens him that everything is already decided, that his opposition won't matter. But Tom, as the seaman is called, won't give in to cajolery: "'As sure as God sees me, I'd sooner lose my hand. If I turn agin my dooty—'" Silver kills him, after striking him from behind with his crutch, but not before he looks at him: "his eye a mere pinpoint in his big face, but gleaming like a crumb of glass." This is the look of hate.

Jim is overcome: "I do not know what it rightly is to faint, but I do know that for the next little while the whole world swam away from before me in a whirling mist; Silver and the birds, and the tall Spy-glass hill-top, going round and round and topsy-turvy before my eyes. . . . Everything else was unchanged, the sun still shining mercilessly on the steaming marsh and the tall pinnacle of the mountain, and I could scarce persuade myself that murder had been actually done."

I have often thought hard about this passage. I have read *Treasure Island* a dozen times over the years, and I have never forgotten that phrase about those eyes like pinpoints. As a child I saw that violence had to have that kind of face. And it astonishes us that after what happens that everything can remain the same and the sun continues to shine in the same way that it did before. Everything passes on, even crimes. The most dramatic events take place in a time no different from that in which normal everyday occurrences happen. And so?

And so you will see this violence often, Francesco, too often. Although your mother and I will try to make sure you don't, you'll see it on television. You'll glimpse it when you flip through channels with the remote control. Dreadful faces with bloodthirsty eyes will flash before your own eyes. You'll find yourself watching American television films that have little to offer educationally. But these things are not the same. The imagination does not get the upper hand and you do not picture anything you do not actually see. Everything is on the surface. *Treasure Island* has often been filmed and been shown on television. I can remember some versions: a blond Long John Silver who is agile on his crutch; a lively, adventurous Jim; and a Dr. Livesey who is authoritative, calm, and very determined. In large part, they all corresponded with my imagination. But then we come to a block: in books there can be smells, in films there are none. Dr. Livesey looks at the island: "I observed the doctor sniffing and sniffing, like someone tasting a bad egg./ 'I don't know about treasure,' he said, 'but I'll stake my wig there's fever here.'" It's true, Francesco, that the "smell of sodden leaves and rotted tree trunks" is something you won't be able to sense from any film. I think you'll soon learn that.

But let's get back to Jim. He falls in a swoon and grows up, just like everyone else. But Jim does so well before everyone else. There is no shortage of eulogies for John Silver, he was the only faithful and honest man among the seamen, and nobody could have doubted his willingness. He acts with a courteous and genial manner towards Jim. He always has a kind and respectful word for everybody. He is exceptional in his shrewdness and opportunism. Stevenson is artful at changing register at just the right moment, turning him in seconds into a monster. First, he reveals the man's background and we come to know his past deeds, but in such a way that his crimes are related with a coldness and cynicism that mask the horror. Only when his game is out in the open, when they disembark from the ship onto the island, and into the novel's true arena, does Silver's blade become a match for his sharp and piercing eyes.

I mentioned that the island is an arena, a necessary setting where everything is corrupted in that region of harsh mountains and putrefying swamps where fever dwells. Jim has only a few minutes to roam about before the first of many tragedies occurs. But despite this, Jim's spirit of adventure and his recklessness save the lives of his companions, the few honest sailors who were never part of the terrible Flint's pirate fleet. And yet despite this, Jim experiences the bitterness of things incomplete, even at the close of his adventure, when the treasure has been found and the pirates overcome. Even after many years, the adventure will remain for him a kind of deep anxiety, and the island a nightmare. Why? Perhaps because he risked losing his life at the hands of pirates? Or, because he came to find that adventures are a source of danger rather than adventure? No, Francesco, the reason is because all the pieces of the jigsaw puzzle fall back into place except one. Once, as a joke, I said that John Silver was like Count St. Germain[2]. Like him, Silver seems to be ageless, to appear out of nowhere, and then to vanish back into nothing. He could even be a devil come among mortal men. John Silver is imponderable, Francesco, the man with whom things just do not add up. He's likeable, yet he's cruel; he's also skillful at changing the cards on the table at the last moment; and he would betray anybody. He can shift over from his companions to his enemies, and then betray his enemies for his own sake. And all this can happen in a few moments, in a flash, and registers in the expression of his eyes.

Francesco, you will read of a desperate struggle on the treasure isle in which there is a whole series of reversals: Silver becomes head of the pirates, Jim is taken prisoner, and yet is saved by Silver. You will read many pages about Jim as he goes adrift in the canoe of Ben Gunn, the man marooned on the island; and how he wins his struggle with Israel Hands, despite his pistols having damp powder and suffering a dagger wound to his back. You will read about all these things, but you must not miss two vital aspects.

Do you remember in the *Jungle Book* how Kaa the snake hypnotizes Mowgli and Bagheera? Well, bear this in mind when reading the end of *Treasure Island*, because here all the signs become confused: we even brush against magic, with specters and ancient evil memories of murder evoked, but nevertheless Silver stands out very clearly governing a difficult situation in magisterial fashion.

And so we come to the final act. It seems that John Silver has won. He has possession of the map of the island which shows the treasure. Together with a few honest men, Dr. Livesey and Squire Trelawney appear to have disappeared, and Jim has been taken prisoner by Silver. Early one morning, taking Jim along with them, the pirates start on their march to find the place where old Flint buried his enormous hoard of treasure, the ill-gotten gains from hundreds of boardings: "We had thus proceeded for about half a mile, and were approaching the brow of the plateau, when the man upon the farthest left began to cry aloud, as if in terror. Shout after shout came from him, and the others began to run in his direction." The pirate cries out because he has found the skeleton of a man who looks to have been a pirate, lying there in an unnatural position: "the man lay perfectly straight." Silver intuits that the skeleton is not there by chance. Its position indicates the direction in which the treasure lies. Silver thinks of Flint: "This is one of his jokes, and no mistake. Him and these six was alone here, he killed 'em, every man; and this one he hauled here and laid down by compass, shiver my timbers!" A collective anguish follows. Overcome by horror, the pirates are like children: they all begin to remember Flint and can't think clearly. A pirate called Morgan says: "'I saw him dead with these here dead-lights. . . . Billy took me in. There he laid, with penny-pieces on his eyes.'" Another recalls: "'Dead—ay, sure enough he's dead and gone below . . . but if ever sperrit walked, it would be Flint's. Dear heart, but he died bad, did Flint!'" And yet another adds: "'Ay, that he did . . . now he raged, and now he hollered for the rum, and now he sang. 'Fifteen Men' were his only song, mates; and I tell you true, I never rightly liked to hear it since.'"

You see, Francesco, how pirates are? They're always talking about money. And when their greatest (today, you'd say legendary) buccaneer dies, they put pennies on his eyes. Be suspicious of people who think too much of money, because they are often pirates in their own way, and not always in disguise.

And yet, at the same time, they're afraid of ghosts. Listening to their horror-struck conversation, Jim gives vent to a sarcastic comment: "the pirates . . . kept side by side and spoke with bated breath. The terror of the dead buccaneer had fallen on their spirits."

That's exactly it. In the following chapter Stevenson completes his masterpiece, closing the novel with great artistry. In reality, Francesco, the treasure is no longer where it should be, having been carried off by Ben Gunn, one of Flint's pirates who had been marooned on the island many years before. Dr. Livesey and the others know this and that is the reason why they gave the map showing the treasure over to their enemies. Silver has the same suspicions, but Jim not at all. Suddenly, at this point, a strange voice—"thin, high, trembling"—comes through the trees, intoning the famous words:

> "Fifteen men on the dead man's chest—
>   Yo-ho-ho, and a bottle of rum!"

At this, all the pirates are thrown off balance. One cries out that the voice is Flint. But the shrill voice belongs to Ben Gunn, who has delivered up the treasure to Dr. Livesey and now wants to place the last remaining pirates in a trap. Together with the marooned man are Livesey, Trelawney, and the others, all ready with their muskets. The voice in the trees has its effect, especially as Ben Gunn mentions names and episodes which only the pirates could have known. But the terror only lasts a short time. Silver recognizes Gunn's voice and the pirates take heart. They realize it isn't the ghost of Flint come to curse them and gradually the thought of the money returns to take the upper hand: the seven hundred thousand pounds in gold buried there and their greed for it replaces their fear of the supernatural. Stevenson is abundantly clear: "The thought of the money, as they drew nearer, swallowed up their previous terrors. Their eyes burned in their heads; their feet grew speedier and lighter; their whole soul was bound up in that fortune, that whole lifetime of extravagance and pleasure, that lay waiting there for each one of them." And does this affect the very shrewd John Silver? Even he, Francesco, the most prudent of all the pirates, the one with the brains, who "can speak like a book," is caught up by it: "Silver hobbled, grunting, on his crutch; his nostrils stood out and quivered; he cursed like a madman when the flies settled on his hot and shiny countenance . . . and, from time to time, [he] turned his eyes upon me with a deadly look . . . In the immediate nearness of the gold, all else had been forgotten; his promise and the doctor's warning were both things of the past; and I could not doubt that he hoped to seize upon the treasure, find and board the Hispaniola under cover of night, cut every honest throat about that island, and sail away as he had at first intended, laden with crimes and riches."

But the macabre illusion soon ends when a strangled cry reveals a large hole, a broken pick-axe shaft, and several boards from packing cases. There, where the treasure once lay, not even one of the seven hundred thousand pounds is left. And here comes the dramatic climax: "There was never such an overturn in this world. Each of these six men was as though he had been struck. But with Silver the blow passed almost instantly. Every thought of his soul had been set full-stretch, like a racer, on that money; well, he was brought up in a single second, dead; and he kept his head, found his temper, and changed his plan before the others had time to realize the disappointment."

You can feel a mixture of admiration and horror for a man as exceptional as Long John. You can be attracted by his talents at the same time you try to forget his more terrible aspects. In life, dear Francesco, knowing how to refrain from the temptation to admire is a difficult art, but an important one. John Silver isn't simply a scoundrel or a criminal who also knows how to cultivate a likeable side; he's not even an ordinary double-crosser, or obvious turncoat; he is something much more like life or the world when its shows its true face: he is anxiety, complexity, the fourth dimension, and the immorality that floats without sinking on the waters of common sense. Having understood that the treasure is no longer there, Silver turns to Jim: "'Jim,' he whispered, 'take that, and stand by for trouble.'/ And he passed me a double-barrelled pistol . . . His looks were now quite friendly; and I was so revolted at these constant changes, that I could not forbear whispering, 'So you've changed sides again.'"

It is the umpteenth betrayal. The last, or almost the last. Jim is indignant. In his place, you'd be too, Francesco. The person who changes allegiance, who betrays, who always goes over to the other side when it suits them, is a person to be reviled. But don't be taken in by appearances. John Silver is a director, not a victim. He doesn't hobble along behind the victors. He's the first to read the situation and arranges it so that the victors follow him. For this reason, you shouldn't put your faith in people like Long John Silver, Francesco, although you won't meet many people like him for the world is made up of very ordinary people who are very different from Silver and more like the silly pirates, felons, or fourth-rate buccaneers incapable of making any decision by themselves. Silver despises them: "'Dig away, boys,' said Silver, with the coolest insolence; 'you'll find some pig-nuts and I shouldn't wonder.'" There's not much point in telling you how it all ends, Francesco. Jim and Silver, alone against the pirates and their rage at not finding any treasure, come out of it unscathed, with the help of Dr. Livesey, the ship's captain, Squire Trelawney, and Ben Gunn, the maroon. Armed to the teeth, they put the four half-wits of pirates to flight.

That is the only way it could end, isn't it, Francesco? It could only end with the victory of the good over the wicked, of the honest men over the pirates, even if victory was bought dearly. But even this time, don't be too sure of who wins. Listen how it really ends. Let's hear Stevenson himself, or rather one of his characters, Squire Trelawney: "'John Silver,' he said, 'you're a prodigious villain and an impostor—a monstrous impostor, sir. I am told I am not to prosecute you. Well, then, I will not. But the dead men, sir, hang about your neck like millstones.'" And how does Silver respond? In the most predictable fashion: "'Thank you kindly, sir,' replied Long John, again saluting."

It is John Silver who wins, Francesco; people like him always win, on condition that they melt away. If you can, you should keep well away from such people. The struggle against them is never easy. The struggle against ambiguity, the dark side of life, that which isn't open and clearly demarcated, is the most difficult. That evening, with the adventure story on the island of treasure having come to an end, the few survivors dine happily together. The story has a happy ending, all things considered. John Silver is able to adjust at once: "'Come back to do my dooty, sir,'" he says to the captain; and we see him "sitting back almost out of the firelight, but eating heartily, prompt to spring forward when anything was wanted, even joining in our laughter—the same bland, polite, obsequious seaman of the voyage out."

There is no history book, Francesco, nor treatise, nor essay, that could tell you more about the human spirit; there's nothing on television that could have you understand it any better, not even when the news shows its hard-hitting and disturbing scenes. Sometimes, when shown with music, those scenes can convey emotions, but literature is different. The other day, a sleepy Sunday afternoon, we were watching the television together. On Channel One they were showing a performance of Mozart's *Requiem Mass* broadcast from the ruins of a library in Sarajevo, and conducted by Zubin Mehta. At the "Confutatis" you were transfixed, dazzled and for half-an-hour you were stock still. Then, when there was a pause in the music you asked, "Daddy, la-la?"—that is, "when will the music come back again?" You were slightly concerned. Something extraordinary was happening, you couldn't tear yourself away for any reason from the images of orchestra, chorus, and also from the superimposed images of the children of Mostar, Sarajevo, and the women of Bosnia. Being only two years old, what will you have understood of all that? What will you have heard in the "Lacrimosa"? I have no idea.

But what I do know is that Sarajevo is full of people like Pew and Black Dog who obey only exceptional and dangerous men like John Silver.[3] Pew and Black Dog end up tried and condemned. Justice is done. But, in the end, people like John Silver get away with it all. Stevenson clearly knows this and has Silver escape, helped by Ben Gunn who shows an attitude of profound respect towards Silver, if not exactly of terror: "[Gunn] had connived at his escape in a shore boat some hours ago, and he now assured us he had only done so to preserve our lives, which would certainly have been forfeit if 'that man with the one leg had stayed aboard.' But this was not all. [Silver] had not gone empty-handed. He had cut through a bulkhead unobserved, and had removed one of the sacks of coin, worth, perhaps, three or four hundred guineas, to help him in his further wanderings."

Silver disappears with a part of the booty, albeit a small part. Nothing more will be heard of him. "Of Silver we have heard no more. That formidable seafaring man with one leg has at last gone clean out of my life," says Jim. This is on the last page of the novel, and, in a way, upturns the conventions of the standard adventure tale, which the narrative of this book, until this moment, seemed to have followed. Jim's adventure is over, thanks be to God. He knows it and knows that he has grown up, paying a heavy price for it. The island, that which everyone thought of as an island of dreams, is now far away. Jim no longer has any doubts: "Oxen and wain ropes would not bring me back again to that accursed island; and the worst dreams that ever I have are when I hear the surf booming about its coasts, or start upright in bed, with the sharp voice of Captain Flint still ringing in my ears: 'Pieces of eight! pieces of eight!'" Now don't get confused here, Francesco, the Captain Flint who utters "Pieces of eight!" this time is Silver's parrot, named after the terrible pirate, and the words that the parrot repeats are the gold coins that are counted out after the bloodshed of the boardings. But notice also the words of Jim: the "oxen and wain ropes," the "accursed island," his "worst dreams" and when he "start[s] upright in bed." The final sentence in which these words are found leaves no room for doubt: Jim's adventure is truly over. His life will now be the same as everyone else's. He will now leave his childhood behind him as if it had been a disease from which he had to recover. And perhaps he hasn't even realized how important it has been for him to learn to survive on the island of treasure. Jim and his friends are saved by his excess of imagination. He is aware of this himself and speaks of the "mad notions that contributed so much to save our lives." In the course of the story there were many mad notions that came into Jim's mind. And it was fortunate that they did. Perhaps the boy's naivete was needed in order to save them all from the pirates' greed and ferocity. But this is a question I'll leave open for you, Francesco. Childhood and adolescence are the time for mad notions. But then it's only been an island, albeit "accursed," and a man, a seaman with one leg, the worst man of all, who disappears. Learn from it, Francesco. Learn from Jim's adventures and his mad notions. And know that when you're grown up you will never miss the island of treasure. Other things, perhaps, but never that . . .

TENDERNESS

There is a strange story, Francesco, that comes from far away. It tells of children who play in an immense field of rye that stands on the edge of a cliff. They play very happily without knowing the danger that lies very close to them. Every so often one of the children—and there are a good many of them—runs the risk of falling over the edge of that cliff. It is at this point that the "catcher in the rye" intervenes, catching the child in mid-air and stopping it from falling. It's a strange story, Francesco, which comes from a misquoted line of Robert Burns, the great Scottish poet, in the confused memory of a character in a book by J. D. Salinger, the American author. In the last chapter I explained to you how life dangles from an ambiguous thread and continually swings between what is right and what is wrong. I told you about Long John Silver, Blind Pew, Black Dog, and Dr. Livesey. I tried to put you on your guard about the most dangerous kind of men, those who don't reveal themselves in the usual kind of way. Now I want to teach you that you can also be a little more trusting. You should know, Francesco, that there can be a "catcher" present who's always ready to catch you when you're playing in the field of rye, because under that cliff live men like John Silver.

The Catcher in the Rye is the title of a famous novel by J. D. Salinger. In Italian, this title couldn't be translated literally because of its references and the complex word-play. A "catcher" can also refer to a player in baseball, America's most popular sport, and "rye" refers not only to the cereal, but also to a type of whiskey. As the Italian edition points out, a translation of the title could also be something like "the fullback in the whiskey (or grappa)." Therefore, in order to avoid any misunderstanding, the novel in Italian is simply called *Young Holden* (*Il giovane Holden*). A plain title, and a misguided one, although there are plenty of plain titles in literature and literary translations. I'll explain later how this Italian title has come to influence the novel's interpretation. As you remember, I said that with *The Catcher in the Rye* we would talk about transgression and about why one should be transgressive. By the end, however, we will see that Salinger's novel isn't only the story of a young man who wants to break all the rules, but something much more: it's the story of an ironical young man who is lost in a sea of rye that borders on a cliff where there aren't many catchers. It is a novel about an adolescent who is desperately seeking a measure of generosity and is virtually a treatise against self-centeredness and an intolerant world, where mediocrity passes for greatness and rhetoric serves to hide smallmindedness of every kind. It's a great book, Francesco, because once again it seems as if it is written in a simple manner. But you have been warned about appearances. Salinger has to be read between the lines, and many distinctions need to be made.

What, then, is the story of Holden Caulfield? It is called a *bildungsroman,* that is, a "novel about growing up." It is the account of a boy, similar in every way to the story of Jim Hawkins, except there are no pirates, no cruel seamen—at least, not in appearance—and it is set in the United States at the beginning of the 1950s rather than the cold of England or the warm Caribbean in the eighteenth century. Both these novels are adventure stories concerning a main character who has to face a series of trials and who decides to relate them. But one only needs a brief glance at the opening of the novels to see that Salinger's style is completely different: "If you really want to hear about it, the first thing you'll probably want to know is where I was born, . . . and all that David Copperfield kind of crap, but I don't feel like going into it . . . "

Immediately we're faced with a transgression, like a slap in the face, right at the start. "If you really want to hear about it," he begins, as if to say: "are you really sure you want to read this book? You really don't have anything else to do?" And he continues, "the first thing you'll probably want to know is where I was born . . . and all . . . " Here, too, there's a huge ironic stance toward literature and the usual pleasure of narration.

Treasure Island opens completely differently: "Squire Trelawny, Dr. Livesey, and the rest of these gentlemen having asked me to write down the whole particulars about Treasure Island, from the beginning to the end, keeping nothing back but the bearings of the island . . . I take up my pen in the year of grace 17—, and go back to the time when my father. . . . "

The difference is not only one of style, Francesco, but one of content. Before he assumes his role of narrator, Holden first has to distance himself from all that is approved, serious and also, in the end, dominant in his culture.

I'd like to pause a moment here, Francesco, and look back to something that happened some time ago. You remember the ancient English teacher I talked about earlier? Well, one day he came into the classroom, which was a modern one with formica tables and a blackboard fixed to the wall. He signed the register, took off his glasses, put his hands in his trouser pockets, and stepped down off the dais. This was the sign that we would be talking about literature, rather than having a language lesson. It was a sign we were often given. "Have you ever heard of J. D. Salinger?" he asked, in his croaky voice—the result of the filterless French cigarettes he smoked. We had not yet heard of him, but what soon impressed us more than the book was the figure of its author, whose only photographs in circulation were taken when he was a boy, and who lived like a hermit in some woods in New Hampshire. And just when literary circles in America were celebrating him as one of their greatest living writers, he disappeared—suddenly one day—as if he were a willful child playing a nasty trick. He decided he wouldn't give even another line to his publisher and would fire cartridges filled with rock salt over the heads of any reporters and snooping photographers.

The fact that Salinger decided not to publish anything further and would not even speak to anyone is a real mystery that no newspaper nor conjecture could even begin to approach, let alone reveal. He is still writing today, even though no one knows what, nor why he does it, and naturally no one knows what will become of the manuscript. But when Aldo (my ancient English teacher) asked us if we knew J. D. Salinger, we jumped to read that book with its large blue square on the cover, making it look so plain, and with no information about the author—not even his date of birth. I discovered later that it was the author himself who had created a worldwide ban on any information about himself and who would not even allow any introductions to be written for any of his novels. Salinger wrote this, his first novel, in the 1940s, and published it in 1951. We were reading it in 1977. A difference of twenty-six years. When Salinger published it there was no Vietnam, no President Kennedy, no dream of Martin Luther King, and Malcolm X was still a young man, to say nothing of the Berkeley campus which was still a highly respectable place where the students all paid their fees and wore collared shirts and ties. But Holden Caulfield was in that world and very much in evidence. Then Salinger began to slide away and to hide behind his characters—such as Phoebe, Seymour, Franny, and Zooey—whom he sent out into the world as a way of gaining time, while he escaped. They kept the public occupied for him; it was a little like the author of a theatrical piece who, cloaked by the darkness, blocks the exit from the theater until the performance is over.

But those mornings, when Aldo told us about Holden and, possibly, about Salinger (I can't tell today, it seems as if an entire century has passed and yet it is only twenty years), we were fascinated by the character's vitality and language. The book seemed to have been written in the future rather than the past. But we still couldn't understand Salinger's retreat, nor his madness; that escaped us. Adolescence is a time of total adherence to the world: you want to be everywhere at the same moment, you try to be everywhere at once like a water diviner searching through the desert. For us it was bizarre of Salinger to go off and hide himself at exactly the moment when things were becoming successful for him.

"Have you ever heard of Holden Caulfield?" my teacher would ask the more reluctant students. He used to tease them, knowing they had no idea who Holden Caulfield was while they, completely unaware of the maieutic system, certainly had no idea they didn't know. We looked down on our classmates with an air of superiority and just a hint of snobbery. And that was right. Salinger himself would have approved. He was the man our class described as "this suave, handsome, sophisticated New Yorker in his single-breasted overcoat (one with a velvet collar). . . . " We'd never seen anything like that. He gave the impression of having *been around* more than any of us. His brusque and sarcastic manner captivated us.

Can you begin to see why I've chosen this story for you, Francesco? You can see that books refer us back to personal histories. All books give this possibility: they are interpretative machines endowed with a conscience, which is yours, the reader. This is why books are wonderful, they allow for different interpretations; they're only opened by keys which you have to search for, or which chance drops into your hand when you least expect it. Books don't open up for everybody, and less for those who don't even search. And it will happen that you will come across books you will not succeed in opening up interpretatively, because you won't be able to find the key. It has often happened to me. I've had to abandon books, even important ones, like *Madame Bovary* or *The Leopard,* among others I could mention.

Life is composed of revelations, epiphanies. I'm relating my epiphanies to you here, and in them there is sure to be the recollection of a book (that I've later re-read many times), but also the memory of the circumstances in which the book was first read. Holden's experience was my adolescence, his transgression was my transgression. Reading about Holden for me was the discovery of sarcasm and irony. It was also understanding that the world is composed of many ordinary respectable people, even when they don't seem ordinary in any way, and who even appear out of the ordinary to others.

It was also to understand the nature of intelligence, curiosity, inspiration, and desire—the overwhelming desire to catch everyone off their guard and really argue with them. Who in a debate would have the courage to say that Flaubert was a writer of negligible importance? Or that Mozart was an unjustly overrated composer? Who would have the courage to maintain that the prose of a writer like Grazia Deledda was uneven, or that poets like Quasimodo were simply full of banality, or that Pier Paolo Pasolini's novels were boring and run-of-the-mill?[1] No one. It has been more than one generation that's been taught to bow down before the constituent authority of the ruling culture, consisting of the masterpieces and the stimulating books, but only those by the great authors, where *A* is only for Aretino, *B* is only for Bontempelli, *C* is only for Contini, *D* is only for Dumas.[2] They're all great writers, and all their works the same. But sometimes there's the need to say that we don't really need to bother with Shakespeare's *Titus Andronicus,* or that Gianfranco Contini's critical apparatus for Montale's *Ossi di seppia*[3] (which can deliberate over missing commas) can leave one cold and is certainly no help in understanding the text. You feel this need because of the uncritical way that Shakespeare is Shakespeare, Contini is Contini, and even Dante can't be touched . . . all of him, canticle after canticle, tercet after tercet, rhyme after rhyme, as if it were something absolutely perfect, written without any concessions—because genius never makes any mistakes—and, above all, never gives way to anything. But when everything is considered perfect, Francesco, it loses its meaning. It's like the league tables for soccer. When the list is short and all teams are at the top, it's confusing. But, taken by six-month periods, the history of literature multiplies the numbers present exponentially and so rightfully pushes the old members, the classics, to the top of the table. They'll tell you, Francesco, how important it is to read the classics, and how you mustn't skip them so that you won't be depriving yourself. This is an obsession of cultures that are weak: don't let yourself be influenced, Francesco, read what appeals to you as long as you have a critical method. And here Holden Caulfield can help you, with that way he has of addressing the reader, that way he has of setting everything alight on a single page.

This is a story which Holden should not be telling, because it's not good, because the morals of American society won't allow it. But immediately he turns around on himself and says, "I'll just tell you about this madman stuff that happened to me around last Christmas . . ." He tells us that he has shared his story with his brother D. B., a screenwriter who makes a lot of money. Holden seems to resent his brother's commercial success.

I'll pause here, Francesco. Holden has it in for everyone, even for the success of a brother who was first a true writer and is now someone who "prostitutes" himself in Hollywood. But there is something measured about Salinger's style. It has a cutting quality, something difficult to apprehend: a style that is apparently simple, apparently candid, and yet, between the lines, leaves glimpses of deep suffering. It is always like that with great books. You have the feeling that everything is comprehendible, until you realize it actually isn't. To give it a sporting analogy, it's like those trick shots in soccer where the ball seems to be curving straight towards you, so you can deadball it, but then it curves away in a different direction. It is the same with Holden Caulfield, who is not any likeable anti-authoritarian kid, but an elusive character; elusive precisely when it comes to summing him up, when you think you know everything about him. The same kind of feeling happens in life with friends, women and all . . . and it is a good sign. It means that the touch of presumption that all children and adolescents display has faded away, and you will come to understand that the meaning of what is happening can elude you, even when you don't think so. It is also the same with good writing. You have to chase after it continually, and it is good for you to do it.

You have to chase after Salinger's characters, beginning with Holden. After having openly said he has no wish to say anything about his personal history, he then begins to tell us all about his boarding school, Pencey Prep, and how the school pretends to be something it is not with magazine ads that show a "hot-shot guy" playing polo.

Holden is a difficult character, Francesco, with many sides to him, like John Silver. Every line delivers a judgment on the world, every paragraph is an opportunity to tell us all about everything he doesn't like. Holden gives us a glimpse of what it's really like at Pencey Institute: "It was the last game of the year, and you were supposed to commit suicide or something if old Pencey didn't win." Holden, of course, isn't the kind who's going to "commit suicide" if Pencey doesn't win; he isn't the kind who derives much profit from being there at all; he doesn't have a good relationship with his parents, his teachers, his girlfriends, nor with the rest of the world. He's a misfit, not a hero worthy of imitation, although you might wish to keep an eye on him, because through him you can understand the taste for desecration, especially today when sacred things are nothing (we'll discuss this later, when looking at Eliot, and it'll be yet another way, different again, for understanding how—forgive the term—the sacred has been emptied of significance).

Just when it's Christmas, Holden is expelled from Pencey for flunking his subjects. Instead of going home, he decides to wander aimlessly around New York. He wants to escape the wrath of his parents for having been kicked out of school. The shame of it! They'll be "pretty irritated," writes Salinger. But one should not be too taken by the way Holden expresses himself: it's a winning way that, over the years, has become the property of many young people who imitate Holden, perhaps without knowing it. But that is a minor matter to consider. One should really be aware of Salinger's more important messages to the reader. In the very opening pages, Salinger has Holden say: ". . . I'm seventeen now, and sometimes I act like I'm about thirteen. . . . Everybody says that, especially my father. It's partly true, too, but it isn't *all* true. People always think something's *all* true."

The italics here aren't mine, they're Salinger's. They underline a great truth that Holden is fully aware of at only seventeen. People always do think something's *all* true. And a little later, he says, "People never notice anything." This isn't a negligible statement, Francesco. You could even consider it a fundamental philosophical principle, a rule of life.

At the same time, it is also a bitter observation. The conflict between Holden and the rest of the world begins here, precisely from his critical method, from this argument *on* a critical method. Everything else follows from this. But when you deal with simplification, when you deal with sound common sense, which in the end explains everything, you equally run the risk of not being understood. All this is part of the American mentality. But by the time you are grown up, Francesco, perhaps that will be our way of thinking as well. Take the first few pages, for example, where Holden speaks about "clear" ideas, about things being "true" and of "molding" youth. Always be suspicious when someone says to you that they always have clear ideas, when they boast about knowing a truth that holds true for everything. But also be wary of those who say there are many truths. It is better to start from this presupposition: truths are never total, they are always partial, and always imperfect. Holden, in fact, has such a fear of indubitable truth that he says he's a terrific liar, even about the most basic things such as claiming to go to the opera when he's really going to buy a magazine. He tells us, "It's terrible."

Perhaps not exactly terrible, although one shouldn't do, or say, such things. Holden comes to understand this later, when his trouble starts to hit him. *The Catcher in the Rye* goes by the name of an entertaining book, and a stimulating one, which it is. But it is also a bitter one; one where childhood and adolescence become fused in a kind of guilt. An important Italian philosopher, Benedetto Croce, once said, "The young? All they have to do is wait to grow old." He was wrong. There's a time for everything. Don't ever forget this.

But let's get back to Holden: he's disoriented. His parents sent him away to a prep school so that he would come out of it with clear ideas, but he's thrown out precisely because he refuses to have clear ideas in the way they want. Now, Francesco, I don't mean to say that whoever wants to protest is right, and that whoever refuses to accept authority is also right. Life is a subtle mix of things: it's not only made of transgression, and it's not only made of obedience. Nor is it made up solely of irony, in the same way that it's not solely empty rhetoric. Being an Italian child, you will probably not be going away to school—Italian children don't—so you'll have less obligations and fewer constraints. But if you don't let yourself be taken in by the "hot-shot guys" who go horse jumping, it will be due to books such as the ones I'm talking to you about. If, at certain moments, you feel the world is full of people who "aren't listening to you," and you are able to put up with it, it will be precisely because you will have been prepared for it. *The Catcher in the Rye* is certainly a book about transgression, but it's much more a book about childhood, when the child looks at the adult world and judges it with a kind of resigned condescension. Holden, who is already an adolescent, does it, but so does Phoebe, his younger sister who is only ten and whom Holden holds very dear: "I mean if you tell old Phoebe something, she knows exactly what the hell you're talking about." Holden's tone changes when he comes to speak of his sister. Or of his brother Allie, who died of leukemia, and who wrote poems on his baseball mitt so that while he was waiting for the pitch he could read a few lines.

You see, Francesco, Allie played the position of a *catcher* in baseball, exactly like the *catcher* in the title, who saves all the children who might fall over the cliff on the edge of the field of rye. Holden always carries Allie's mitt with its poetry everywhere with him.

He takes it with him even on his wanderings around New York, when he decides not to go home for a few days, before he has to tell his parents that he's been thrown out of Pencey for not applying himself. In reality, he's running away, running away from everything—except from Allie, who's already there with him, and from Phoebe, whom he wants to telephone immediately when he gets there. But that's not possible because it is too late at night.

So he gives up that idea and takes a room in a hotel with its own nightclub inside. Then he calls Jane, an old friend. Together they go to another nightclub, called Ernie's, in Greenwich Village that his brother D. B. used to go to before he moved to Hollywood. Then, with the help of a hotel porter, he has a prostitute sent up to his room. But things don't go as they should. Holden doesn't really give a damn about the girl, and the porter, whose name is Maurice, wants extra money for his trouble. Holden doesn't oblige and ends up with a painful punch in his stomach.

The book seems to run along the usual lines, and it is entertaining; except there is a dialogue between Holden and a taxi driver named Horwitz that I'd like to look at more closely:

> "Hey, Horwitz," I said, "You ever pass by the lagoon in Central Park? Down by Central Park South?"
>
> "The *what*?"
>
> "The lagoon. That little lake, like, there. Where the ducks are. You know."
>
> "Yeah, what about it?"
>
> "Well, you know the ducks that swim around in it? In the springtime and all? Do you happen to know where they go in the wintertime, by any chance?"
>
> "Where *who* goes?"
>
> "The ducks. Do you know, by any chance? I mean does somebody come around in a truck or something and take them away, or do they fly away by themselves—go south or something?"
>
> Old Horwitz turned all the way round and looked at me. He was a very impatient-type guy. He wasn't a bad guy, though. "How the hell should I know?" he said. "How the hell should I know a stupid thing like that?"

The conversation continues and Holden questions the fate of the fish that live in the lagoon. The taxi driver responds, "They live right *in* the goddam ice. It's their nature, for Chrissake. They get frozen right in one position for the whole winter."

At first I told you that the book may seem to be entertaining and—above all—light, except for the apparently casual pages and chance digressions, like this one about the ducks in Central Park. What does it matter to Holden Caulfield where the ducks go in winter? And yet he is obsessed by it. He has already asked the first taxi-driver who'd taken him to the hotel, and heard the following reply: "'What're ya tryna do, bud?' he said, 'Kid me?'" Holden tries again with the second taxi driver, Horwitz, who is more willing to discuss it. Look at the italics used by Salinger here: "'The *what*?'" referring to the lagoon; "'where *who* goes?'" referring to the ducks.

It doesn't take much to realize that neither really cares about the ducks in Central Park at all. Not only this, but the question is actually an irritating one: who could ever care about the ducks on the lagoon? And what of the fish who could starve to death if the lake froze up in winter? They can't die of hunger, they can't not find food: they have *pores*, that's their *nature*. If a child can't find a balance in a world of grownups who take no notice of him, if he doesn't manage to be caught by the *Catcher* in time, what would happen to him? Nothing at all. They're all like the fish: "'They live right *in* the goddam ice . . . They got their *pores* open the whole time. That's their *nature* . . .'"

Have faith in Salinger, Francesco. You'll like his other books as well. It is strange that a man so extraordinarily preoccupied with people's fates in the world, who pays such attention to the smallest and largest details at the same time, should have decided to publish nothing more. It is strange that the author of a book such as this has not felt the necessity or need to ask himself again where the ducks go in winter. My suspicion is that he suddenly found out and discovered that— in a frozen city like New York, where the taxi drivers think you're crazy if you're worried about the ducks—they don't know where to go. But let's not get distracted, Francesco, and continue with our reading, because *The Catcher in the Rye* has further surprises for us.

Later, hoping to meet his kid sister Phoebe, who might be there on a school visit, Holden goes off to the Museum of Natural History. There, with a disarming naturalness, he reflects on the passage of time: "The best thing, though, in that museum was that everything always stayed right where it was. Nobody'd move. . . . Nobody'd be different. The only thing that would be different would be *you*."

He then transfers the same thoughts over to his sister and reflects on how she inevitably must "be different" as well. He would prefer it to be otherwise, however: "Certain things they should stay the way they are."

This is about melancholy, Francesco. Do you remember in *Peter Pan* when Wendy's father decides that the following night she can't sleep with her little brothers because she's grown up? And what does Peter Pan say when Wendy tells him that from the following day she must be grown up? He says no, and in order to avoid it, he'll take her to Never Land. Well, this is a little like that, Francesco. Holden suffers from the fact that little Phoebe will grow up and won't be simply a "really smart" kid anymore. Basically, Holden's days in New

York before going home are a little like Wendy's in Never Land. When he gets home, Holden will have to grow up. And growing up for Holden will be so painful as to leave deep scars, even in his physical makeup. I don't want to say that such pain and suffering always accompanies growing up and becoming an adult, fortunately it doesn't. But it does for Holden because, out of all the children, he is the one who is about to fall over the cliff. Even if he is nearly eighteen, he is still the child who desperately hopes that the catcher will get hold of him as he falls. And it happens: he will be caught. But, in the meantime, Holden has the chance to look over the edge and he understands the risk he runs and—even more—how he's running it. And so, without letting his parents know he's there, he goes home one night with the intention of talking with Phoebe. He doesn't wake her immediately, but wanders about the room, reading through her exercise books and notes.

After amusing himself leafing through his sister's stuff ("I felt swell, for a change . . . I just felt good."), the notes she'd made in school, her clothes in order, he decides to wake her. Phoebe is happy, but surprised to see him. But she understands that Holden has been kicked out of school and fears their parents' reaction.

It's during this midnight chat with his sister that Holden asks her about a Robert Burns poem:

"You know that song 'If a body catch a body comin' through the rye'? I'd like—"

"It's 'If a body *meet* a body coming through the rye'!" old Phoebe said. . . .

"Anyway, I keep picturing all these little kids playing some game in this big field of rye and all. Thousands of little kids, and nobody's around—nobody big, I mean—except me. And I'm standing on the edge of some crazy cliff. What I have to do, I have to catch everybody if they start to go over the cliff—I mean if they're running and they don't look where they're going I have to come out from somewhere and *catch* them. That's all I'd do all day. I'd just be the catcher in the rye and all. I know it's crazy, but that's the only thing I'd really like to be. I know it's crazy."

Here is the story of the catcher, the nucleus of the novel and the source of its title. Of course, it doesn't translate into Italian. For us in Italy, Holden's transgression is a precursor of 1968, a sort of protest *ante litteram,* a proto-desecrator of the system, of the social values of America of his day. This is true, Holden is a young rebel. But I assure you that all that came afterwards, and came about precisely because Salinger conceived of a world saved by children. It's true that Holden rebels against Pencey, its teachers, and the puffed-up snobs of his friends. It's true he's ironical about everything that's happening around him: this is because everything happening around him runs along the same predictable—and even a little stupid—lines (remember the phrase "People always think something's *all* true"). Holden's problem is that everyone drinks martinis, everyone has an opinion about everything, but not about the ducks. His problem is not that he can't quote Robert Burns correctly, but in having to distort it, in order to draw from it a moral, a desire, and a rule of life.

At the end of the book there are several extraordinary passages, such as when Holden and Phoebe go to the zoo together. Holden is about to go home, but first—with an excuse—he goes to Phoebe's school to pick her up. In their usual fashion, they walk and talk together. Then they arrive at a carousel. Holden sits on a bench and Phoebe has a ride. I can well remember the first time I put you on a carousel, Francesco. It was a very beautiful one, such as you don't see very often, quite an old one made up only of horses. You were on the back of one of them, clutching its neck and almost hugging it. You were really excited. I noticed that because your eyes were more luminous than ever. You were a little over a year old. There were no other children, and it was a strange hour of the summer night—eight o'clock perhaps, when the artificial lights mingle with the twilight—which gave an unusual appearance to everything. I was watching you with a mixture of curiosity and emotion. I had to make an effort to remember what music it was they were playing. It was not the usual old waltz, but a number from an old film (old even for me), called *Sabrina*. Two characters played by William Holden and Audrey Hepburn dance to this music. It was a beautiful feeling there. Perhaps the same that Holden describes when he sees his sister on the carousel: "I felt so damn happy all of a sudden, the way old Phoebe kept going around and around."

This is the novel's last scene. The last chapter (26) is only one page long and explains what happens next. An epilogue that's perhaps inevitable.

There's a psychoanalyst who asks him many "stupid" questions about how Holden plans to behave at school next September. And his brother D. B. is nearly as bad because he asks Holden what he thinks about the most recent events of his life. "If you want to know the truth, I don't *know* what I think about it." Once again Holden gives a lesson in critical method: he puts everything in doubt, including enthusiasm. He chooses not to give conclusions, nor any judgments. It's extraordinary how at the same time this book succeeds in being a fierce criticism of society and also a great lesson in tolerance. Holden takes everything on his shoulders, but makes no protest. Even little Phoebe risks falling into the trap at the end and almost gives in to the temptation to judge her brother. But he simply says, "I don't *know* what I think about it" and the word *know* in italics says a great deal about Salinger's intended meaning. The last page of *The Catcher in the Rye* is full of understanding towards the world: the comprehension of someone who has paid and knows how to make everyone else pay. But there is an underlying melancholy: "I'm sorry I told so many people about it. About all I know is, I sort of *miss* everybody I told about . . . I think I even miss that goddam Maurice."

You see how all Holden's caustic irony melts away in a second, Francesco? How that word *miss* is put in italics once again by Salinger? A period that will be unrepeatable for

Holden is now over. Growing up has a price that, right up to the end, Holden has tried not to pay. There's an entertaining singer/songwriter called Paolo Conte who, once in a while, I let you hear. In one of his songs, *Boogie,* there's a line which says, "It was an adult world, we made professional mistakes." Growing up means that you change your way of looking at the world and even your way of making mistakes. It's not always a good thing, but it's always necessary. The important thing, dear Francesco, is to know that somewhere there's some catcher in an enormous field of rye who's ready to save the children—those at least—before they fall over that crazy precipice. It's only a dream against all the stupid realities with which Holden continually has to deal. But it was useful to him, and it can also be useful to you, even if later, sometime, in dreaming too much, you become melancholy, like that melancholia of the novel's last words: "It's funny. Don't ever tell anybody anything. If you do, you start missing everybody." And it's true, Francesco.

PASSION

Don't ever tell anybody anything. If you do, you'll start missing them. But can we miss characters—who are only imaginary creations—whom we only come face-to-face with, as it were, in a poem? You can certainly miss Holden Caulfield, but what about the gentleman who descends the stair in *Prufrock and Other Observations*? And the women in the room who come and go? They will tell you it is not possible, Francesco. And some readers—few, I hope—will wonder at me for having picked from the shelf one of the most difficult, certainly one of the most complex, books of modern literature, T.S. Eliot's *Collected Poems*. But this isn't the way to look at it, Francesco. Remember what I said to you earlier: do not think of literature as an unreachably high mountain. Well, this is a good chapter for putting that view into practice, because now we are going to talk about poetry. And we will do it not so much because poetry ennobles the soul, and helps us delight in the world, but also because it enables us to understand it better. They will tell you that poets are like musicians; that poetry is great when it has musicality, a light touch, rhythm, and a recognizable structure. You will be taught about Italian meters like the octosyllabic couplet, the hendecasyllable, and how to recognize the sirima of a canzone. At school, you will be taught what catachresis is, how to tell a tercet from a quatrain, and you will also come to learn the meters of Latin poetry. You will enjoy memorizing certain lines of poetry, because of the way they sound, such as these from Dante's *Inferno* (XXVII, ll. 61–66):

> S'io credesse che mia risposta fosse
> A persona che mai tornasse al mondo
> Questa fiamma staria senza più scosse.
>
> Ma percioché giammai di questo fondo
> Non tornò vivo alcun, s'i odo il vero,
> Senza tema d'infamia ti rispondo.

["If I thought my reply were to a person who would never return to the world, this flame would be without further movement./ But seeing that from this deep pit no one has ever returned alive, if what I hear is true, I will respond to you without fear of infamy."]

This, Francesco, is from Dante's *Divine Comedy*, but it is also from Eliot, being the epigraph to one of his longer poems, "The Love Song of J. Alfred Prufrock," that I want to tell you about here. It's a strange title, isn't it? Poems usually have simple titles, like "To Sylvia" (*A Silvia*), "The Albatross" (*L'Albatros*), or "The Sepulchres" (*I Sepolchri*)[1]. This one sounds traditional enough, but it is rather too detailed. Is that "Alfred" really necessary? Wouldn't it have been enough to call it "The Love Song of J. Prufrock"? Or better still, "Love Poem"? Perhaps it might have been, who knows? But in this poem the complications are not only in the title or the choice of epigraph. It is a difficult poem because it is about a difficult man, about what this man should do (and doesn't) every day, and about what happens in the world and has been happening for some time. It is a poem about the things of this world, which are often small things. And all this comes together—as can only happen with poetry—in one great poem. If, my dear Francesco, somebody says that poetry, literature, and even philosophy, is far too complex and is only trying to show off, you can respond with the example of Eliot. He is a poet who has turned complexity into an exercise of simplicity—even when he writes about the Tarot, Dante, the Holy Grail, and goodness knows what else—because you can tell somebody about it all and understand it all, on condition that you are intellectually honest. You cannot simplify anything. And to divulge something to people is synonymous precisely with communication and transmission, and nothing more.

Today you were playing in the park, Francesco. You took your animals, your giraffe—the tall one—, your lions, and your three elephants—the largest one and the two smaller ones. You were speaking to them and changed your voice as you brought each character into play, giving them a script to follow that you created. You are beginning to do it quite a lot, and one day I hope you will come to have a passion for the theater.

But before returning to Eliot, Francesco, before reading "Prufrock" (and then "The Waste Land"), I would first like to make a digression on the theater. I will not be talking about the texts of any plays in this book. I had thought about Luigi Pirandello's *I giganti della montagna* ("The Mountain Giants"), but it would have taken us too far away from my themes. Many years ago (although not that many), I knew a man named Ennio Dollfus. He was performing in a late show in a bar in some remote district on the outskirts of Alessandria, late in the evening, perhaps even after midnight. Ennio Dollfus was a hard, terse man who bragged about his Alsace origins and about being related distantly to the Austrian chancellor who opposed Hitler. But he also had a flow of eloquence, sometimes a veritable stream of it, which was often cynical, worldly-wise, and yet witty. I first met him as he was biting into a hot, spicy sandwich, eating at the late, irregular times kept by actors, acrobats, and even lion tamers, perhaps, (yes, I will be taking you to the circus soon, Francesco, very soon). He was speaking of the past; his words seemed to come from way back, as experienced actors know how to do. He mixed—in the same breath and with the same dignity— quotations from Shakespeare and from lesser mortals, while creating a strange digest of opinion, but all in an extremely distinctive and lively manner. For years Ennio had been artistic director of the local theater company, *I Pochi* ("The Few").

That is what the company called itself, a little ironically. But they were not just a bunch of amateurs. I had heard of them at home because they used to talk about an aunt of mine who had performed in Tennessee Williams's *The Glass Menagerie.* That must have been in the 1950s, those vibrant years after the war that touched even a province in the south of Piedmont, which otherwise seemed so remote from it all. There in those years, when education was for the very few and when there was scarcely any culture and little drama—but a great deal of light entertainment—somebody came out of the heart of Europe (at least, I like to think of it like this) to a coastal plain thick with fog, in order to bring *theater* to it, just as Colonel Aureliano Buendia in *One Hundred Years of Solitude* is taken out and learns what ice is.

Alessandria must have been dreadful in those years: flat, sprawling (having lost its fortifications), with no narrow winding streets, and no river running through the heart of it. It had no mysteries whatsoever, nor any legends worth the name. It really was a dreadful place, and run down, too, with no splendors. In the once great Borsalino factory, the sirens were now dead. The factory, over a twenty-year period, had transformed the local population by giving work to women at that time when they usually did not work in factories, and brought an elegance to streets which were still country style and downhome.

What a man from Alsace was doing in those streets I have never been able to find out. I know he was there because he was still there when I met him all those years later. He was in the theater, his theater, one without the sanctity of a prayer meeting or the mistakes that locals make, and without the lunacies and sham theatricalities of the so-called avant-garde. His theater had a certain detachment, with a hint of fatalism about it. And, in spite of themselves, the citizens of Alessandria came to learn how to perform Eugene Ionesco, Luigi Pirandello, Albert Camus, and later Bertolt Brecht, Anton Chekhov, Carlo Goldoni, Jean Anouilh, and Antonin Artaud. Many people passed through Ennio's "school" with its unwritten rules, its subdued lighting, its squeaky floorboards during rehearsals, and its costumes mended once too often. Some members passed through by chance, or only briefly, without having the time to hope for anything greater, such as Milan's Piccolo Teatro, or even further afield. Others quickly thought of something else to do, a more reputable job, one where you can eat at regular hours, and go to bed when everybody else does; one that carries no risk of becoming an obsession, nor tugs at the coattails of great spirits of the past, nor has to live with any ambiguities of the dramatic text. Some passed through as one crosses the stage, with barely time to hear the noise their feet made echoing through the empty theater. Thinking back on it, I realize that Ennio Dollfus was actually writing the city's "unofficial" history (that is the term, Francesco), its outwardly less well-known history. And it is a disquieting history for me because it is unresolved. It is too obvious, too practical, and, in the end, too empty a city. Alessandria is like a music of ideas that fades like an old shellac disc that is about to come to an end, yet with none of the empty horror and ugliness of a small town that forces you to leave because it is a desert, its soil one in which nothing can grow. You will understand better below why I'm telling you this crazy story of a provincial city: this is not simply a digression, Francesco, there is a meaning to it. Alessandria is a provincial city, but it is not that far away, like a Samarkand in reverse, a photographic negative, distant from everything and reached only on horseback with plenty of supplies, the good fortune of passable roads and no wild animals to molest you. There are places, Francesco, and Alessandria—the city where I was born—is one of them, which are like a glutinous spider's web: they stick to you in a protective kind of way. It is not easy to escape from Alessandria because it is a place that is directly in the middle, not far away from anywhere else, but distant enough from other ideas. It is a city of the Enlightenment, but still incapable of delighting in its own clear reason, like French cities or the people of Lombardy. It is ugly, although without the awful speculative buildings found in other cities; and sleepy, but—unlike the suburbs of the larger cities—with no actual dormitory towns. In a subdued, low-key way, it is even cultured. It doesn't smile a great deal, but then it is not sad, like that proud sadness many faces in the South have. Even melancholia isn't a thing of these parts: that is considered to be a decadent emotion, the "spleen" shown by desperate people, something only for those with a debt to their memories, or those with nothing better to do.

I Pochi must have been something for those with nothing better to do: they were actors who never even chose the great plays, the grand style, or the immortal authors. With Ennio, you didn't play Shakespeare. Shakespeare was too great, too imposing, too important, and with too many acts. Ennio preferred neutral tones, pastel tints: Camille Pissaro and Edgar Degas, rather than Eugène Delacroix. And besides, through those streets unchanged over the years (except for the tramlines which no longer exist), less explicit and more ambiguous and subtle suggestions emerge. It must have taken some effort not to have become resigned to being a middling kind of place, and to press down on the accelerator of the passions, regardless. Although Alessandria is a wise city, it is suffocating and somewhat boring, like a textbook on civic education. Leafing through the stifling pages of those books, you are struck by the grayish print, as faint as that of a badly printed brochure. You are also struck by the measured quality, from which a Baudelaire, a Radiguet[2], a Wilde, or a Hemingway could never have been born. All the way from Alsace, Ennio must have known it was quite a gamble, that it wasn't a question of reawakening souls—like some good shepherd of the theater—but of eliminating those neat fences, that ordered, lucid setting, and the antiseptic clinical smell that wound through the streets when the wind blew.

I think he did succeed in bringing people to the theater, and it is thanks to him that I, too, learned to love the theater; and to his discretion in not wanting to impose the emotions, in not wanting to make it a gospel for anybody and everybody. In fact, many people remained unconverted, and there is nothing wrong with not going to the theater and missing its magic ability to make scenes seem real. You can live just as well, quite well, without the theater. But you have to understand, Francesco, that I did grow up better because of it. It was an education to peep down, almost hidden, on those floodlit stages during rehearsals, listening to the actors recite in low hesitant voices. The theater is something I love, along with music and literature. One more reason for writing these pages is because of these loves, in the hope that, whatever it is you wish to do in life, you will understand that the dimension of the dream, the story, the fantastic, will not be given to you by just anybody and that an enriched life is one that is not able to do without it. The more the world tells you that all these things are superfluous, the more you should apply yourself to considering them a part of life.

But we have not made this digression solely in order to tell you how one learns to love the theater and how important it is to meet certain kinds of people; there is another motive that will bring us back to Eliot. You play a lot, Francesco, and give voices to the characters you invent, making them recite your words. I have told you about a city that has never succeeded in having a taste for the theater, that has never loved the idea of the *fabula*, the tale, or the literary world; that has always abused its own sense of measure, balance, and grayness. I've told you about a city that has never dared to disturb the universe, just like the character of Prufrock. But it didn't do so out of idleness, and certainly not out of respect or fear. This character called J. Alfred Prufrock that is placed under observation by the fastidious Eliot (the collection from which the poem comes is called, appropriately, *Prufrock and Other Observations*) is not a man who dares not disturb anything because of idleness or disillusionment: he does not dare because he simply fears the consequences of his actions. He knows that action—even if, at first sight, it might appear very small—could move a mountain. And at this point, Francesco, you will be asking yourself: what kind of action do we mean here? But you must be patient, we will get to that point in time, and if you follow closely, you will not be let down.

How does "Prufrock" begin? With a grand panorama:

> Let us go then, you and I,
> When the evening is spread out against the sky
> Like a patient etherized upon a table;
> Let us go, through certain half-deserted streets,
> The muttering retreats
> Of restless nights in one-night cheap hotels
> And sawdust restaurants with oyster-shells:
> Streets that follow like a tedious argument
> Of insidious intent
> To lead you to an overwhelming question . . .

Can you catch the smell of the city's urban decay? Look closely at the lines, they're nothing like those they will teach you about in your first years at school. They have none of the lightness of, say, Lorenzo the Magnificent, nor the "spleen" of a Baudelaire, nor that *maudite* air like Dino Campana ("Nella notte fantasiosa,/ Pur mi sento nella bocca/ La saliva disgustosa. Via dal tanfo/ Via dal tanfo e per le strade . . ." : "In the fantastical night,/ I still feel in my mouth/ The saliva of disgust. The stench of the road/ The stench of the road and through the streets.").[3] And it's very distant from Beckett's cult of the absurd ("dragging his hunger through the sky/of my skull shell of sky and earth"). No, Eliot's poem has something very different: his lines are as cold as the lights along an expressway intersection, where the glow comes not from the stars in the sky but from reflecting lights. Nor do they hark back to myths or primitive rites: they are about as wretched and as contemporary as they can possibly be. When Eliot begins with those two lines, he knows exactly how to create a contrast. It could be the beginning of virtually any poem, the story of two people who, one evening . . . But, of course, this isn't the case. It is Prufrock speaking to himself, to his conscience. There is no one else with him. And then it comes as a surprise that the evening which is spread out against the sky is likened to "a patient etherized upon a table." This would be a patient under an anesthetic who is about to undergo an operation. There is nothing colder than this image, and nothing more surprising. Eliot opens with his warm invitation of "Let us go then, you and I," and before that there is the epigraph I mentioned before: "S'io credesse che mai . . ." (When you go to school, Francesco, your teacher will explain that this is *Inferno* Canto XXVII, where Guido da Montefeltro confides to Dante the terrible sin that has brought him there, and will only do so because he is certain that his words will never leave the confines of Hell; thus he will only speak his heart to a person who will never return to the world). All this leads up to that cold image of a man anesthetized. And not only to that, but to:

> The muttering retreats
> Of restless nights in one-night cheap hotels
> And sawdust restaurants with oyster-shells

Can you see the contrast, Francesco? At one and the same time, for Eliot, our world is the direct descendent of Dante Alighieri and also the product of a world which has lost its conscience with regard to the value of actions and things. Eliot's poem was written in 1917. I'm writing this in 1994, so that a little under eighty years have passed, but not so you would notice. When you are grown up, you will read the newspapers, watch television, follow political debates, and listen to intellectuals who will try to explain what is happening in the world, and why, and in what manner. But to really understand the times we live in, you only have to read a few lines of poetry written nearly eighty years ago. You only have to look at the contrast between Dante and a man whose consciousness has been wiped out by an anesthetic, and the "retreats" that are "muttering," where no words reach you except that muttering. And the places are not homes or houses but—note—"retreats" and "hotels," places where you spend "One night" and where that night is "restless." And the restaurants? Sawdust mingled with oyster-shells: the garbage of luxury. And even "the streets which follow like a tedious argument" are useless and boring. And yet we live in a world organized by streets: you will go by means of them, drive down them, and walk down them. Our whole life, Francesco, is organized by way of *streets*. The other day, on the airplane bringing us back to Rome, you were looking out of the window and pointed out to me the distant network of lines you can see from up there. They looked like a tangled skein of threads, but they were roads, some wide, some thin, some with sharp twists. From airplanes you can see not only the countryside, but all the agglomerations of cities and the white threads of roads—those which Eliot followed like a tedious argument: here, in all this, in this turbid thought where oyster shells, the table where the patient lies, the cheap one-night hotels, come to dominate an ordinary evening sky. Then, at the end of this road, comes the refrain, like a kind of jingle:

> In the room the women come and go
> Talking of Michelangelo

Do these lines seem obscure to you? Has there been a leap of logic? Does it seem as if these two lines have nothing to do with the lowlife theme of the poem, with that atmosphere both muted and decadent at the same time? No, they have a lot to do with it, Francesco, and very much so. Do not have any faith in people who will tell you that speech must always have unquestionable logic. Do not have any faith in people who cannot put up with the fact that, in order to understand something, it is sometimes necessary to have a mental short circuit. The experts in communication studies say it is only normal to see Ingrid Bergman and Humphrey Bogart having a dramatic discussion while a twin-engine aircraft taxis along a misty runway in that blue-gray color that only old black-and-white films have, and then, only a second later, find yourself steeped in bright color with a smiling family singing an advertising jingle. Nevertheless, in a flash you understand that *Casablanca* has been interrupted to give air space to a company that, at the least opportune moment, wishes to explain why you should buy a product filled with cheese that needs frying. The trouble here is that it isn't an intellectually dangerous leap of logic. Eliot's is, of course: something for people with time on their hands. But that's not it, Francesco, you have to make an effort here! These two lines of poetry are really easier to understand than the instruction manual of one of those idiotic remote-controlled airplanes. Why do the women come and go talking of Michelangelo? Because they symbolize the vulgarity of our age. Eliot was something of a snob, and a class-conscious one at that; he couldn't bear people talking about one of the greatest geniuses of all time while coming and going through a room, busy—perhaps—with other things (who knows what those women were doing "in the room": sewing? shelling peas? cooking meatballs?). But don't take it too literally, Francesco. Eliot means to say that in a world as degraded as the one he lived in (in which we also live; eighty years later, it's still the same), even Michelangelo risks becoming a subject as cheap as a "one-night" room where you smell the odor of oyster-shells and sawdust. It is the same for Michelangelo, as for Dante, and for the Bible, they don't much matter. You can see now what a rich meaning emerges, and without it being complicated.

Let us look at the next stanza:

> The yellow fog that rubs its back upon the window-
> panes,
> The yellow smoke that rubs its muzzle on the window-
> panes
> Licked its tongue into the corners of the evening,
> Lingered upon the pools that stand in drains,
> Let fall upon its back the soot that falls from
> chimneys,
> Slipped by the terrace, made a sudden leap,
> And seeing that it was a soft October night,
> Curled once about the house, and fell asleep.

What does this mean, Francesco? Is it simply the description of a London scene? Or something more? The writing is very fine. As a boy, I loved this stanza very much because I was born in a place where the fog is thick and yellow and rubs its back against the windowpanes. It's true. Being a child in Rome you know little about fog. In Rome the windows of the houses are usually open because there is never any shortage of sunshine. But I lived my adolescence out under the sign of winter. By that I mean that living in the northern cities means living in winter; my memories are more of winter than spring or summer, because the autumns and winters there are full of colors, burning reds, and vermilions, sometimes even purples. And the gray's never a simple gray, it's more ash, pearl- or iron-gray. And the yellow fog that Eliot writes about here is not saffron or gold (such as the flower of broom), but rather a pale straw color. Colors aren't the same for everybody. You can almost recognize poets by the way they use colors. Eliot's colors are foggy, smoke-yellow, with white lights. In this "Love Song" everything is nebulous and immobile. The only thing that moves in this poem is the smoke that licks the corners with its tongue and lingers over the drains. There is almost a wish to be protected, to look out on the external world from a secure, closed place. The fog, which can rise up anywhere, can only rub its back against the windowpanes, and nothing more; it rises over drains, in the corners of the evening, but not where Mr. Prufrock is—no, not there. He can stay calm because nothing outside can touch him. And even if this is so, there will be time:

> And indeed there will be time
> For the yellow smoke that slides along the street
> Rubbing its back upon the window-panes;
> There will be time, there will be time
> To prepare a face to meet the faces that you meet;
> There will be time to murder and create,
> And time for all the works and days of hands
> That lift and drop a question on your plate;
> Time for you and time for me,
> And time yet for a hundred indecisions,

And for a hundred visions and revisions,
Before the taking of a toast and tea.

Here is the fear, Francesco, Prufrock's terrible incapacity
to make any decision about anything. It's as if he were a wisp
of that smoke, that yellow fog that, squeezing in everywhere,
seems to go nowhere in the end. Can you see now, Francesco,
how even modern poetry can be transparently clear? In this
poem there is a continual sense of loss. "There will be time,
there will be time," says Prufrock, repeating the word: time
for a hundred indecisions, visions and revisions, before the
taking of a toast and tea. Is this simply a poeticism, Francesco? Not a bit of it. That toast and tea is a very precise
image. It is how Mr. Prufrock imagines himself next to the
person to whom he doesn't dare make his declaration of love.
Taking tea is never a chance thing; it is one way to mix the
small things of everyday life with the large. Mr. Prufrock has
a secret he can't admit, which is a real and true sin: the fear of
revealing himself. That is the reason why Eliot put the epigraph of Dante's Guido da Montefeltro. You remember it?

Ma perciocché giammai di questo fondo
Non tornò vivo alcun, s'i odo il vero,
Senza tema d'infamia ti rispondo.

["But seeing that from this deep pit no one has ever returned alive, if what I hear is true, I will respond to you
without fear of infamy."]

This secret, this sin, is so inadmissible that Prufrock can only relate it on one condition, the same as Guido da Montefeltro. He can only tell it to his own conscience ("Let us go then, you and I . . ."), and to no one else. And all this simply for a declaration of love, Francesco? All this complex poem to tell us about a certain man named Prufrock—not even a pleasant name, if one thinks seriously about it—who has no talents, no particular qualities, and who must be in love—mildly—with some female neighbor to whom he dare not speak a word? Oh, come on now, someone will say to you, what about the other activities of the human spirit? What about the scientists, or the economists who tell you how to become rich, or the great engineers who build bridges? How about the statesmen, celebrated lawyers, fearless judges, surgeons who transplant hearts, livers and kidneys? Or the men who fight for peace, the diplomats who avert wars, the rare responsible politicians who actually think of their country? These are difficult times; it seems the well-read are never of any use. And to think this T. S. Eliot even won the Nobel Prize for Literature! Well, Francesco, if any person who thinks they are cultured and fairly well-read says anything to you—even remotely—resembling what I have just written, you know you can disregard it completely. And remember, even lawyers, economists, and physicians can only be good lawyers, economists, and physicians if they have truly learned how to read a great poem. If they can't, they're only hacks, extremely mediocre ones.

But let us return to Prufrock, to "there will be time" and those two repeated lines about the women who come and go, talking of Michelangelo, and those indecisions and revisions. It is important to understand, Francesco, how skilled Eliot is at creating the inconsistency of contemporary life; how life's big decisions end up by simply helping us take a toast and tea. And it is important to understand that it is so. Actions, aspirations, and dreams are never measured in size, and they do not always have anything to do with what we call an objective. Poor Prufrock, this gentleman who is turning a little gray, has dreamed of fulfilling a deed, and has been stopped by lack of courage—the courage to change the established order, the courage to change the logic of things. The American television films you often watch (sometimes too often) will show you a succession of powerful men, bosses of their own worlds, men ready to push fateful buttons to set off wars, nuclear explosions, and I don't know what else. These films try to teach you that decisions are always linked to something huge, inexorable, and important. Poor Prufrock has nothing huge to decide, no wars or anything else: he makes no decisions and that's it. But he knows what he should do and he also knows the decision has no meaning for anyone else but himself. Yet he still can't do it; he puts it off, then debates with himself about it, only to put it off again:

And indeed there will be time
To wonder, 'Do I dare?' and, 'Do I dare?'

Time to turn back and descend the stair,
With a bald spot in the middle of my hair—
[They will say: 'How his hair is growing thin!']
My morning coat, my collar mounting firmly to the
    chin,
My necktie rich and modest, but asserted by a simple
    pin—
[They will say: 'But how his arms and legs are thin!']
Do I dare
Disturb the universe?
In a minute there is time
For decisions and revisions which a minute will
    reverse.

Why disturb the universe, Francesco? What does "'Do I
dare?' and 'Do I dare?'" mean? Dare do what? The critical
guides won't enlighten you, Francesco. They will tell you (as
I read somewhere) that this poem is a sort of contemporary
hell, a hell into which Eliot has descended in order to tell us a
drama; some even talk of the "time of the Fall." You can forget them. You will come to understand by yourself, and I'm
sure you are capable of it, how much academic essays are
really worth, and how many books by critics are written solely
for winning awards or for showing how much more intelligent the critic is than the author. Dear Francesco, you can
forget what the specialists will tell you. The subject matter
here is very simple: Prufrock doesn't dare make a declaration
of love, but he thinks about it every day, and this is his sense

of the passing of time. It is not an inexorable time, it is a sense
of sadness, where for him there's always a possibility: "There
will be time, there will be time." That is because the decision
is simple, quick and almost commonplace: "Time to turn
back and descend the stair." And then comes one of Eliot's
many strokes of genius—"With a bald spot in the middle of
my hair." Mr. Prufrock is beginning to grow old while he's
thinking about his insistent question, which never changes.
And then, in parentheses, he immediately adds "[They will
say: 'How his hair is growing thin!']." *They will say,* Francesco. Some lines later there's another analogous phrase:
"[They will say: 'But how his arms and legs are thin!']."
Again, *they will say,* dear Francesco. Prufrock is growing old
in the eyes of others, too; the others who don't know about
him, like Guido da Montefeltro who desires no one alive
should know of his sin ("But seeing that . . . no one has returned alive from this deep pit . . ."). The others who have always noticed only small external signs, will suddenly look at
him—one day, like any other day—and notice he is losing his
hair, his legs are thinner, and that he lives out an existence in
the grayest way: "My morning coat . . . My necktie rich and
modest." Note the difference here, Francesco, between the
adjectives "rich" and "modest." But here the two are to be
equated, because he lives a life of modest richness and modest poverty (but certainly not like the epic image of Pelizza da
Volpedo's *Il Quarto Stato* [4]). And then this Prufrock, with his
hair growing thin, with his good suit and necktie asserted by
a simple pin, this dull and predictable man, who doesn't know

if he'll ever be able to make a declaration of love, overturns this solemn image in two lines:

> In a minute there is time
> For decisions and revisions which a minute will
>   reverse.

Can this be so, Francesco? Is a minute all it takes? It would seem not, it seems only an illusion because, in the end, there is not much to discover: the decisions to be taken won't come to anything we don't know already. And, after asking himself if it would ever be possible to change the course of destinies which, in their modest richness, proclaim themselves equally similar, he then tells you with a touch of resignation:

> For I have known them all already, known them all—
> Have known the evenings, mornings, afternoons,
> I have measured out my life with coffee spoons:
> . . . .
> And I have known the eyes already, known them all—
> The eyes that fix you in a formulated phrase,
> . . . .
> And I have known the arms already, known them all—
> Arms that are braceleted and white and bare
> [But in the lamplight, downed with light brown hair!]
> . . . .
> And should I then presume?
> And how should I begin?

Good heavens, Francesco, what terrible anxieties he has seen and known already! What anxieties can a life measured out with coffee spoons have, given those short minutes, simple and predictable, placed one after the other? And the eyes? Those eyes that fix you in a formulated phrase? What phrase? And what are those arms rich and bare that Prufrock knows so well? And in what evenings has he glimpsed in the lamplight that they're "downed with light brown hair"? It is not worth asking. It is pointless to repeat a play that Prufrock, by now, knows in all its parts. And so this "song of love" becomes a sort of failure, a song that's impossible, except for something else which arises, something only the ambiguity of poetry can really give you. Can a man like Prufrock, measuring out life with coffee spoons, really disturb the universe? Can a man like him ask:

> And would it have been worth it, after all,
> After the cups, the marmalade, the tea,
> Among the porcelain, among some talk of you and me,

Don't be fooled, Francesco; it would've been worth it and without that expression "after all," which Eliot repeats twice, just to underline how thoughtful poor Prufrock really is. I have not chosen this poem for you, Francesco, in order to say "take it as a lesson," or to say to you that it is a good rule to disturb the universe; I chose it to make you understand how great a temptation it is to say, "For I have known them all already." I'm telling you this story in order to say "pay attention," because in the end it will be worth it. Because the ending is in a crescendo, the gloomy crescendo of a man who knows nothing more than to occupy himself with the question "Do I dare?" and who can only remain in "all the butt-ends of my days and ways."

Oh yes, Francesco, beware of the indecision and fear of this terrible love song; the fear of not doing something because in the end, it's all the same, because nothing will ever change and, if it does, it can all change again and again, in a minute, or a second. Learn from it what everyday life is like without any meaning, learn that the yellow fog which rubs its back against the windowpanes can protect you. However, this one terse line should stay in your mind, because it might escape you when the occasion presents itself: "And in short, I was afraid."

Here is his solemn admission. Here is the motive for his lack of action. Here, again, Prufrock is forced to feel sorry for himself and say pathetically:

I grow old . . . I grow old . . .
I shall wear the bottom of my trousers rolled,

Shall I part my hair behind? Do I dare to eat a peach?
I shall wear white flannel trousers, and walk upon the
    beach.
I have heard the mermaids singing, each to each.

I do not think that they will sing to me.

Prufrock is lost. He knows it, but will admit it only to himself. His walk through the semi-deserted streets ends like this, with the mermaids:

> We have lingered in the chambers of the sea
> By sea-girls wreathed with seaweed red and brown
> Till human voices wake us, and we drown.

What is it that our Mr. Prufrock can't tolerate? He can't tolerate the mediocrity of his life, but also that of the world at large. He can't tolerate everything running according to gray rules, and that he is of the same grayness himself; he is incapable of doing even the simplest thing, so things become unreachable for him:

> No! I am not Prince Hamlet, nor was meant to be;
> Am an attendant lord, one that will do
> To swell a progress, start a scene or two,
> Advise the prince; no doubt, an easy tool,
> Deferential, glad to be of use,
> Politic, cautious, and meticulous;
> Full of high sentence, but a bit obtuse;
> At times, indeed, almost ridiculous—
> Almost, at times, the Fool.

When you are older, many people—perhaps too many of them—will tell you that you are living in an age of vulgarity, in an age of ugliness, with bleak housing in poor taste. Someone will tell you also that the ability to *read* beautiful things has also been lost. It is not true. Or rather, it is not always true. Although there are more people born who are destined to "swell a progress, start a scene or two," rather than be Prince Hamlets, that is how it has always been, Francesco.

However, now you can understand the long digression on the theater and Ennio Dollfus who, from far-off Alsace, came to my native city and brought it the theater. A city which—like all cities in the world—is made up of thousands of Prufrocks and no Hamlets; a city where it is easier to ask oneself, "Do I dare?" all one's life than it is to stop the procrastinations once and for all. You see, Francesco, I was born in a strange place, a very strange one: a city neither beautiful nor excessively ugly—one that's both boring and also a little wise. Every so often, with friends who don't know Alessandria, I amuse myself by telling them anecdotes about the city's history, and they're amazed at it. Although founded in 1169, it has conserved almost nothing from the past. There are no great cathedrals, no palaces, and not even—as I mentioned before—a river running through it. The nearest one, the Tanaro, runs to one side, in a marginal way, keeping to itself. One day, some time after the year 1200, St. Francis of Assisi passed through the area and there he met a wolf, one exactly like the famous wolf of Gubbio. Naturally St. Francis tamed the wolf, but it's the one in Gubbio that is the more famous. The good people there, after purposefully constructing and cultivating a mythology about it, have been living off their wolf ever since with tourism and pilgrimages. In Alessandria there is no recollection of St. Francis at all: he was only that strange friar who spoke to animals. One of Alessandria's famous sons, Umberto Eco (who has actually been a great master—as it used to be said—for me), has defined the problem as a "diffidence for the *noumenon*." I can't explain what the *noumenon* is for you here, but, only say that the citizens of Alessandria show a diffidence towards the mysterious, towards anything out of the ordinary. Even the patron saint of the city, San Baudolino, isn't like the others, who all performed miracles. One day a king's son was hit in the eye by an arrow. People ran to tell Baudolino in hopes that he could save him. Baudolino saw the horsemen arriving in a great hurry, but before they could tell him what has occurred, he says he already knows all about it, and is sorry, but there is nothing he can do: the boy will die. The miracle was in his clairvoyant knowledge. As for the clinical aspect, as was clear to everyone, there was little anyone could do. He was made a saint, perhaps, because of his undeniable sense of the realistic.

"I have measured out my life in coffee spoons." I was born in a place where there was an abundance of coffee spoons, and the art of measuring out is very widespread. You, Francesco, were born in Rome, a very different kind of city, where everyone thinks they are Hamlet. Being able to measure the next person by the use of coffee spoons has helped me, especially in my job. It has helped my sense of irony and given me the capacity to keep my distance from things, yet to know the value of others; I am able to bring everything down to the lowest common denominator and never up to the highest common multiple. There is a great deal of difference, Francesco. I hope that you, who will perhaps live in a city of Hamlets, will be able to understand someone who was brought up in a city of Prufrocks. Do you remember Holden Caulfield and Phoebe, his kid sister? There is an extraordinary scene in *The Catcher in the Rye* that I'd like to bring up here and now.

During the days of Holden's peregrinations through New York, before going home, he goes to the theater in the company of Sally, a girl he likes very much. They go to see a play performed by a company that is very much in fashion, very committed, very intelligent, that of the Lunts. Sally runs into someone she probably met "at some phony party" a while ago, and they discuss the play. Holden is disgusted by her friend's remarks about the play, "He said the play itself was no masterpiece, but that the Lunts, of course, were absolute angels. Angels. For Chrissake. *Angels.* That killed me."

I've learned not to trust people who use words like "angel," "extraordinary," "divine," and I don't know what else—and not at the age of thirty-three, but since I was sixteen. Being born in a city where they wouldn't find it extraordinary if a comet fell slap bang in the middle of its historic center has helped me. But leaving it has also helped me, as it has living now in a city where they find even the smallest of fireworks *extraordinary*. I'm not sorry for my excess of disenchantment, it is a solid lesson for life. I only hope that you, little Francesco, can one day understand what it means. In short: learn from Prufrock, but beware of him. If you like, transform him into a Prince Hamlet, and liberate him from those damned questions of his. You will meet men and women who go across a room, an airport lounge, a conference hall, talking of Michelangelo, talking rubbish, and trivializing. You will have to put up with them, but you must also judge them, and without listening to too many appeals. I hope you will be able to disturb the universe even if, sometimes, it seems small to you, really very small, and even if that universe seems not to have any interest for anyone else.

Yes, Francesco, I hope you never have to say: "And in short, I was afraid."

So now I've also told you about fear. When John Silver kills the seaman who refuses to sell his soul to the pirates, or when Pew comes, announcing himself by the tapping of his stick on the frozen pavement, I've told you about real, disquieting fear. But this fear of Prufrock's is an entirely different matter. Physical courage isn't enough to overcome it. You need another kind, the kind you will have to construct—or rather, fortify yourself with—over time. But this will not be easy for you, because you will often find that there is a desert around you and because often the actions of your life will appear to be empty, with no value, like those of Prufrock. Also because one day you will descend that stair, and worry a little about what others are saying, and arrive at a moment (and it will be a good deal sooner than you think, and much more illusory than you might imagine, and you will have to change your mind immediately), a moment in which you seem to have seen everything before, in which boredom will overcome you. And in that moment you will remember not only Prufrock, but also "The Waste Land."

❋ ❋ ❋

When you are forced to listen to empty phrases, to a worldliness without any real values, the false extraordinary accounts of ordinary men, then—I say, then—your mind will come back to the opening lines of "The Waste Land":

> April is the cruellest month, breeding
> Lilacs out of the dead land, mixing
> Memory and desire, stirring
> Dull roots with spring rain.
> Winter kept us warm, covering
> Earth in forgetful snow, feeding
> A little life with dried tubers.

It is one of the most famous opening passages in literature. April is cruel because it subjects nature—its roots, flowers, and even dried tubers—to rebirth in a world where nothing has any value. And if, at the start of April—the month in which you were born, Francesco—nature reawakens, that doesn't mean it is the same for the fashionable cosmopolitan world which Eliot presents to us within the lines immediately following:

> Summer surprised us, coming over the Starnbergersee
> With a shower of rain; we stopped in the colonnade,

And went on in sunlight, into the Hofgarten,
And drank coffee, and talked for an hour.
Bin gar keine Russin, stamm' aus Litauen, echt
    deutsch.
And when we were children, staying at the arch-
    duke's,
My cousin's, he took me out on a sled,
And I was frightened. He said, Marie,
Marie, hold on tight. And down we went.
In the mountains, there you feel free.
I read, much of the night, and go south in winter.

Don't worry about the words you don't understand. You will hear many more, whenever you travel. The world is full of people who say "Hold on tight," and "In the mountains, there you feel free." And still others who make things clear (in the way I will translate the German for you now): "I'm not Russian at all, I come from Lithuania, a true German." This is "The Waste Land," a sequence that you can't explain to children because it is too difficult. Even Eliot's first publisher was afraid of its difficulty and asked the poet to write a series of explanatory notes before it was published. Eliot did so, but even today they do not help explain a thing, but complicate it instead. You, on the other hand, Francesco, will understand without too much fuss, and without fear: literature isn't a monolith if it is approached with humility, certainly, but also with determination. The landscape of the "The Waste Land" is the same as that of "Prufrock": one-night cheap hotels, a waste land where Eliot's pessimism came together. You can

feel it in every line. Yet it is not a desperate pessimism; if anything, it is of a more conscious and scornful kind. After having given voice to the aristocrats, who talk about sleds and
lakes, Eliot asks himself:

> What are the roots that clutch, what branches grow
> Out of this stony rubbish? Son of man,
> You cannot say, or guess, for you know only
> A heap of broken images, where the sun beats . . .

Have you noticed how in this poem the tone has changed,
with respect to the poem about Prufrock? It is no longer an
intimate voice, looking through the keyhole at a character
who is looking at his own reflection. Here the gray Mr.
Prufrock leaves his post and, as he himself would have said,
becomes submerged in the crowd. In this chapter of ours he
has recited a few opening bars, then merged back into the
chorus, mingling with the mass of people, a ruin, a root, one
of the many broken images where the sun beats.

You see, Francesco, my passion for "The Waste Land" was
a real obsession. I've thought of writing something, an essay
perhaps, on this poem for a long time. And now here are
some lines to invite you to read Eliot as if he were a lens; yes,
precisely that, a magnifying lens to aid your understanding,
to help you see the world around you more clearly. If you can
do it, you will become aware that those lines can present
you with unexpected reflections. To put it another way, Francesco, think of this sequence as if it were a thermometer, tak-

ing the temperature of an age in crisis. Do you remember how at the beginning of this book I told you about a mysterious woman by the name of Madame Sosostris? We're about to come to her. But contrary to what we've done for Prufrock, where we read almost the whole poem line by line, here I want to make some leaps. We'll cut here and there and move forward in another way. It is a way of reading that certain cultural authorities, blinded by hypocrisy, do not accept. You see, Francesco, there was once a very intelligent gentleman by the name of Samuel Johnson, known to everyone as Dr. Johnson. He was a man famous for the things he said and wrote. Somebody once asked him if you always had to read books from start to finish, and received the following caustic reply: "Why? Do you read books from start to finish?" All those who truly know how to read know that you don't have to read from start to finish. Reading isn't like following a railroad track, you can travel by leaps and bounds, and sometimes you can abandon the reading altogether because what you have already read is quite sufficient. The one question people always ask you is, "But have you read the *whole* of Proust?" And your teachers will tell you that a book isn't read until it has been read from cover to cover. And yet, Francesco, you will leap onto buses halfway through their journey, you catch trains that have begun the journey hours earlier, and enter suddenly into the middle of discussions where you will not know what has already been said, and you will certainly start watching films halfway through. Perhaps you will never ever know if some music heard on the radio or on the street is from its first movement or beginning or not. And this is to say nothing of the remote control for the television which multiplies this effect exponentially. You have begun to use it yourself: when you have seen a film from beginning to end you now prefer to go back to a certain scene that lasts only several minutes. Instead of a complete narrative, you prefer to experience the thrill of one of your favorite scenes again. The same thing happens with poetry. After you have learned a few lines of a poem by heart, you will like reciting those lines and no other, continually, listening to the sound. You will only be doing the same thing as when you watch the scene from *Lady and the Tramp* you love to see over and over again where the two Siamese cats tease the dog. And you do this all by yourself, pressing the rewind button and going back to the start of the scene. So Francesco, I'm going to imitate your own method of going about things. I'm going to take Eliot's poem as if it were one of your cartoon films and go to my favorite lines, those which underlined or accompanied many moments of my adolescence, and which I've recited to myself dozens of times, as if they were a song. Are you ready to do this? Of course you are. So I've chosen the lines on the "hyacinth girl" and the lines on Madame Sosostris. You remember I spoke of her? A certain "clairvoyante" with a strange name? Well, after Eliot has told us that our civilization is "dry stone [which gives] no sound of water," where "the dead tree gives no shelter, the cricket no relief," and after having spoken empty meaningless phrases, the poet introduces the most important theme with the next three lines:

Madame Sosostris, famous clairvoyante,
Had a bad cold, nevertheless
Is known to be the wisest woman in Europe,

In that waste land where slothful specters of men hover—
Eliot says, "I had not thought death had undone so many,"
echoing Dante (his favorite poet)—Madame Sosostris, a vulgar
'clairvoyante' who is ignorant of the ancient mythical game of
the Tarot, passes for the wisest woman in Europe only because
she pretends to know how to use that devilish pack of cards.

You will meet new clairvoyants, Francesco. They often call
themselves "intellectuals" or, today, "communications' men"
or simply "managers" or "writers," or whatever name they
give out. Before you speak to them, look into their eyes and
try to understand if they really know how to read their Tarot
or not. Beware of those men with no memory at all but who
are capable of freely ransacking the texts of previous authors
without any understanding or feeling for them. These new
clairvoyants, who are always referring to the future—of "society," "civilization," "literature," "art"—have come to see the
world of culture as a boring activity, a sideline for idle people
who have no wish to say anything to anybody. Because of
this, when you are grown up, it will often happen that you will
hear it said that a lawyer's more useful than a writer, or an
industrialist more useful than a poet. And only one evening
during some holiday, after having had a good deal to drink,
and they're more disposed to be generous, only then do these
people—who are convinced of the uselessness of any thought

that has no practical application—only then do they tell you that when they were young they once admired books and poetry, and only then will they look benevolently at anyone who earns their living by the pen. Don't be misled by this act of complicity because literature isn't a dream to be kept in a box or in a case on display. It is a discipline, a way of coming to know the world. It requires logic, intuition, and skill. You can write an essay all at one sitting, but not a novel; remember that. It is not inspiration which holds a novel together; only effort, method, and attention to detail can make a book, a collection of poetry, or a short story into a great work. Look at Eliot, look how he is able to make so many digressions, but all of them controlled, woven together, and worked over with the absolute rigor of a skilled artisan. In 1922, when "The Waste Land" was first published, the critics expressed conflicting views. One wrote that a poem which needs footnotes is no different from a painting which underneath tells you, "This is a dog." The same critic also wondered what sense there was in giving a citation from Ovid halfway through a phrase, with no subject or main verb, and omitting even the reference itself and continued: "And when one person hails another on London Bridge as having been with him 'at Mylae', how is the non-classical reader to guess that this is the name of a Punic sea-fight . . . ?"[5]

But you can do this, Francesco, you can. It wasn't allowed then, but today everybody does it. Today no one will explain anything to you for the very good reason that you can't explain anything about works of art without running the risk of limiting them, or even making huge errors. But don't worry about things like that, always ask when you don't understand. Perhaps the explanations will be even more obscure, but that doesn't matter. You should never be afraid of appearing naive. The blackmail of naivety is a power that should have no influence over you, because it is a power that's not worth a penny, and good for nothing at all.

So, why Mylae? you will ask. And I will reply: Mylae isn't only the name of a famous sea battle. In this poem, it is much more. After having portrayed a decaying and desolate picture of the contemporary world and making Madame Sosostris the symbol of its vulgarity, Eliot changes his poetic scenery. It is the same kind of procedure they have in films. Even at your age, you are already familiar with the fact that films are edited and scenes spliced together. Eliot uses the same technique in this poem:

> Unreal city,
> Under the brown fog of a winter dawn,
> A crowd flowed over London Bridge, so many.
> I had not thought death had undone so many.
> . . . .
> There I saw one I knew, and stopped him, crying:
>   'Stetson!
> 'You who were with me in the ships at Mylae!'

We're back with the fog, Francesco. That fog which, like a cat, rubs its back against the windowpanes of Prufrock's house is no longer yellow but brown—the color of a winter dawn. You can't imagine how many times I've seen a fog like that, brown in a winter dawn. And every time I've seen it I think of Eliot's line. Indeed, it was Eliot's line that made me discover the fog. At first, for me, born and brought up in one of the foggiest northern cities, fog was simply a fact of meteorology, and then it became a fact of poetry. Well, in that unreal city where anonymous slothful people pass over London Bridge, the poet meets somebody he knows called Stetson. And who might he be? Stetson is a well-known make of hat in America. In fact, Stetson hats were worn by another great American poet called Ezra Pound, to whom Eliot sent the first draft of "The Waste Land." Pound took up his pen and set about cutting the work down, correcting, and underlining passages he did not find convincing. Eliot used many of Pound's suggestions and thanked him in a dedication after the epigraph which reads: "For Ezra Pound, il miglior fabbro" (which means "the better craftsman"). But his friend is also found in the poem, and they meet again after having been together at Mylae, defending that culture and civilization which both of them embodied.

The naval battle in 260 B.C. at Mylae between the Romans and the Carthaginians was a crucial moment for the history of civilization: it was near Mylae that the Romans were victorious over the "barbarian" Carthaginians. Although more than two thousand years have passed—as in one of the fables I read you before you go to sleep—the two poets Eliot and Ezra Pound are there on those ships. But not only this, you have to connect all this with the beginning of the poem from which I gave you several lines above—which recalls vegetation and fertility rites. Remember? April falls a few days after the spring equinox when plants begin to flower and the earth is reborn, waking up from its long, cocoon-like winter sleep. In an explanatory note, the poet says he owes a debt to two anthropological works, one of which is Sir James Frazer's *The Golden Bough*. This is another of those books that, for years, I often carried around with me and which has helped me understand many things, especially about literature. You see how it all interweaves? Eliot directs you to a writer called Frazer, and Frazer directs you to another, and he directs you on to another, and so on. Do you remember I said to you, Francesco, to watch out because books talk to each other? And they can play tricks. They are always hiding something and keeping it to themselves. The task of finding out what and where it is hidden is up to you. You can play with books as if they were a game on a merry-go-round or hide-and-seek. Books tell stories so that you can make up other stories from them, and sometimes they mingle true stories and fictional ones, giving equal importance to both. That is why Eliot, after giving you his own description of the beginning of spring, then sends you immediately to a text of anthropology. And if you read the pages and chapters of this text which Eliot indicates, what will you find? You will find that the ships at Mylae and the vegetation ceremonies are not separate things, because some years after that famous battle something very important happened in Rome.

In 204 B.C., towards the end of their long struggle against Hannibal, the Carthaginian leader, the Romans adopted the oriental cult of the Phrygian mother goddess because their tired spirits had received a prophecy that gave them some comfort. It said that the Carthaginians, who had actually invaded Italy, would be expelled if the great oriental goddess was brought to Rome. Ambassadors were sent immediately to Pessinus, the holy city of the goddess in Phrygia. And so a small black stone which represented the powerful divinity was entrusted to the Roman ambassadors who took it to Rome where it was received with great respect and placed in the Temple of Victory on the Palatine Hill—which is not far from where we live, Francesco. It was the beginning of April when the goddess arrived, she immediately set to work: in that year there was a harvest more abundant than they had seen in years, and Hannibal and his army of well-experienced soldiers were beaten back and returned to Africa. While he was giving a last look at the Italian coast, which was disappearing in the distance, Hannibal could not have foreseen that Rome, which had fought back against the powers of the East, which he stood for, had actually bowed down to the Eastern divinities.

The black stone representing the divinity was brought to Rome in April. At the very same time, the victory over Hannibal and Carthage was complete and final. The West (which up until that moment still was not "the West") had defeated Carthage, but had given a home to and venerated a powerful Eastern deity. So that during the birth of the West—that West about whose decadence Eliot talks, and of which we are a part of—there was a profound equivocation: that of having driven away the East (in the form of Carthage), while at the same time building a bridge to it by adopting its magic and religion.

I do not want to go any further than this, Francesco. In an earlier draft of this chapter I explained the reason for the opening quotation, taken from Petronius's *Satyricon* and the reason for Tiresias, the seer who was made blind by Juno, and who is one of the many characters who appears in the sequence. An earlier draft also tried to reveal, at least in part, the mystery of the blank card which Madame Sosostris cannot read:

> Here, said she,
> Is your card, the drowned Phoenician Sailor,
> (Those are pearls that were his eyes. Look!)
> Here is Belladonna, the Lady of the Rocks,
> The lady of situations.
> Here is the man with three staves, and here the Wheel
> And here is the one-eyed merchant, and this card,
> Which is blank, is something he carries on his back,
> Which I am forbidden to see . . .

But then I decided against writing about these things. I will leave them for when you have the capacity to absorb them yourself. It would have been like putting you in a helicopter and getting you to the summit that way. When you read a book like *Mount Analogue* you will understand that this method of travel is not effective: that the upward slopes have to be taken step by step. Here I wanted to tell you about the other side of Eliot as well as the other side of Prufrock. I have not spared you quotations, nor complex references, but I have tried to explain things to you in the simplest way possible, which does not mean to say that it is *necessarily simple*.

In the first part of this chapter, Francesco, I told you about the theater, and about the necessity of daring to do things, and I advised you not to have any fear, or rather, never to have the fear that J. Alfred Prufrock has, but rather—if you must have any fear at all—have that of Jim Hawkins. In the second half of this exploration of Eliot, I have tried to make you see that Prufrock's sense of desolation is something much greater: history and its various cultures are mingled together, and the decadence of a world, the outlines of which Eliot already saw in 1922, does not mean that your world will inevitably end in ruins. "The Waste Land" says many things, Francesco, and only stupid people *run out of subject matter*. Among those many things I want you to note, how, in the end, the Romans—even if they were stronger—saved themselves because they knew how to accept the culture of other people and to make it their own. For this reason you should fear the absence of culture altogether, and those people who have no desire to find a language in which to communicate to others. For this reason you should have no faith in those who have no desire to know about their past, be it the battle of Mylae or whatever else.

It will happen that you will often be made aware that the exhibition of ignorance is a vulgar thing. It is not the humility of *I know I don't know*, it is the stupidity of *I don't care anything about knowing*. It is the frame of mind that thinks of "The Waste Land" as a kind of exhaustingly useless intellectual exercise, a mental contortion for people who have nothing better to do. Pay no attention to that kind of opinion, Francesco. Pay attention, instead, to these middle lines of "The Burial of the Dead" in the first part of "The Waste Land," that speak about the hyacinth girl. They refer to a place of love, a desire, perhaps unrequited, perhaps without hope. The atmosphere in these few lines changes, and it is almost joyful. The irritation of empty speech, the desolation of the contemporary world gives way to a memory of a different kind:

> 'You gave me hyacinths first a year ago;
> They called me the hyacinth girl.'

A young woman is speaking as she remembers a happy occasion. But immediately afterward there is a "yet" that overturns that sunny atmosphere and will soon contrast with the brown fog of London Bridge, to say nothing of the grayness of the thinning hair of Mr. Prufrock.

> —Yet when we came back, late, from the hyacinth
>   garden,
> Your arms full, and your hair wet, I could not
> Speak, and my eyes failed, I was neither
> Living nor dead, and I knew nothing,
> Looking into the heart of light, the silence.

That "yet" is the poet's own: these are his words, the description of a failure. Despite her being the image of richness and sensuality—in a word, of beauty—he could not "speak" and his "eyes failed." Is this a negative image, Francesco? Perhaps. But it depends on the reading you give it. The careful explicators of this poem will tell you that this garden is the scene of a love that fails and refers back to the Grail Legend where the impure knight fails in the test, unable to ask the question about the esoteric symbol of the Grail vessel. Very true. But, for me, the hyacinth garden was something very similar to the brown fog of a winter dawn. I was born in the fog, but I did not know it; or rather, I did not know how to express it. And in the unsettling dreams of an adolescent, the desire—or the scene of the desire—became transformed into the hyacinth garden and so became a poetic place. At which point, it is only recently that I have realized that I never knew what a hyacinth was. I would not know how to recognize one. Yet I can deal quite easily with the sacrificial symbolism of the god Hyacinthus.

As you can see, poetry is not always images and does not always refer to something: sometimes it makes you dream of a place whose appearance you don't know but whose unsettling nature you can perceive.

And so this long chapter on Eliot ends here. It ends with the hyacinth girl, and that is how I want it to end. Right from the start I knew those were the last lines I would quote. Why? Because they are accompanied by desire, and not only that for a woman, but for things, objects, and for ideas. We will speak about this directly in the next chapter. There I will tell you about a novel, a film, an emotion, a strange smell of wood, and about talent, as well as the difficulty of living with it, of reading it in others, and of putting up with it in oneself. We will get there in a moment, Francesco, in the time that it takes to turn a page.

TALENT

We have now arrived at the most difficult chapter, Francesco, the one about talent. We have come a long way since the treasure island with its atmosphere of Englishmen and the exotic. Holden and little Phoebe are perhaps having a conversation in some corner of the literary universe (yes, there is a place called the literary universe, where characters on paper speak to each other: I will tell you about it at the end of the book). And in Eliot's waste land, perhaps Mr. Prufrock will be trying to understand why he has never dared. I have always imagined a parallel world where the characters from the world of books look across to our world as if it were a television screen. They sit there together: Ulysses and Madame Bovary, Leopold Bloom and Orlando, Hamlet, Charlus, Renzo and Lucia, Miss Dalloway and William of Baskerville[1]. Every so often another character is added, emerging from some manuscript that has been discovered, or from a newly written novel. Sometimes a real flesh-and-blood character is added to these imaginary figures, knights of literature, people of invention and dreams, because some writer has fished them up and given them the dignity of literature. These real historical people find a new life by being woven into a literary text, something like your ladybug whose story changes every day precisely because it is not a real ladybug. Real ladybugs, more or less, do the same things every day: they fly about, find food, sleep perhaps, and protect themselves from insects who want to eat them. But it is not the same with "your" ladybug, which comes back every day and does something different, like Yanez, Sandokan or the Count of Montecristo. But there are also characters who remain suspended between fiction and reality, without having to give up either side of their identity. They are too large to be simply fictional characters, and even if they were famous, real-life existence isn't enough for them either. In fact, the two roles actually complement each other: the one can't do without the other. However, these characters are rare, Francesco, very rare. But when you find them, the game of literature becomes so fascinating that the fiction which created them, the fiction in which they move, becomes almost secondary and remains almost in the background. This is what happens in Pushkin's short play about Mozart and Salieri, and even more so in *The Loser*, the novel by Thomas Bernhard about the great pianist Glenn Gould.

I had my doubts about introducing you to a novel like Bernhard's which, in many respects, is darkly macabre and, in the end, starkly dramatic. But then I realized that the difficulties came from looking at literature in much too rigid a manner. *The Loser* is a great novel and, precisely because of this, can be read in many different ways. We will look at one particular aspect of the book only, leaving the rest out, and this time our method of procedure will be even more clear. It was less so in the preceding chapters, because I didn't tell you the whole story of *Treasure Island,* and we didn't say that much about the transgressive and non-conformist side of Holden Caulfield. Nor did I explain to you about the Fisher King or Phlebas the Phoenician in "The Waste Land." Here we will not go into the morbid relationship Wertheimer has with his sister, nor the gloomy atmosphere of certain scenes. Instead, we will concentrate on the crystalline notes of Glenn Gould, the pianist who is the true principal character of the novel. Besides, literature has to do with choice, with the desire to take what you wish from a text, be it some parts and not others. The important thing is that the interpretation is sustainable and not arbitrary.

When you watch *Peter Pan,* Francesco, you know very well that Crock the Crocodile circles around Captain Hook's ship because it wants to eat him up. If I said to you that nobody could prove this, that perhaps Crock only wants to play because it was a happy kind of crocodile, you would look at me puzzled, almost in disbelief, and say to me "No, Crock bad." And you would be right, because there is nothing in the text to justify the notion. It is possible that a playful crocodile does exist in a story somewhere, but this *particular* crocodile is *not* playful, as you know very well. The idea that he is playful simply is not sustainable, while your view is the correct one. You should not believe the people who say that texts can be read in any way whatsoever, Francesco, because they don't know what they are talking about. Many people who are "in" books (yes, "in"'s the word they use!) will tell you that interpretations are infinite and say so with a smile and wink of those who want to tell you something and not tell you at the same time. Don't give them any credibility. What they say is like cheating at cards, when you bend the rules to enable a game of solitaire to come out right.

So we will begin with the music, Francesco and—as by now we are accustomed to doing—we will start from a distance, in fact from over twenty-five years ago, in a far-off room in my father's medical office, which was never used, and—as always—in the winter (it is remarkable how everything in the north happens in winter, perhaps because they last so long, or because the summer season is so very hot and changeable that everything has to stop, as if blinded by the light). I remember an old man there, although today I could not say whether he was very old or not—all adults over a certain age seem old to a child because they still have not learned to read a person's age in their face. This particular old man was a piano tuner who was preparing the piano I was to start studying on. It was a German upright piano with ivory keys. I remember it there without its casing, completely dismantled. I saw the hammers which moved at the lightest touch on the keys and all those working parts I later learned to give a name to: jack, escapement spring, support, tape, hammer butt, and hammer rest. They were small working parts in wood, all moving in turn to bring the hammer down on the strings with greater or lesser intensity. The old piano tuner was a craftsman who knew everything about the instrument but not so much about music; he played the piano as they did at one time, old songs composed of lots of notes all piled on top of each other, a musical effect which then I thought acceptable. It would be difficult for me to say today whether he played well or badly, but the thing that struck me, curiously, and that brought me to love music and the piano wasn't the fact that I heard the sound of this instrument when still a small child, but something completely different— something which brings into play one of the other senses, that of smell. What struck me was the smell of wood, the wood of that piano which was a hundred years old. This isn't very strange, Francesco, but something which often happens: you come to love something because of an initial impulse which starts from somewhere completely different. It would have been more usual to have discovered a passion for music by listening to an old recording of Alfred Cortot playing Chopin or Arturo Benedetti Michelangeli's interpretation of Debussy[2]. It would certainly have been the correct impression to pass on to one's children. But, strange as it is, it was the smell of wood, a smell made even warmer by the oil used to polish it. It was a particular, intense smell which only pianos have, even new ones, and which I notice each time I sit down at a keyboard, albeit with some differences.

I really could not say what link there might be between music and the smell of wood, but I think it has to do with the warmth, which gives a sense of protection. But, from that moment on, my relationship with music has been a very intense one, so close that it has helped me to understand better how to read books. When you grow up, I don't know if you will become an engineer, doctor, farmer, or traveling salesman. I don't know how much you will read, or if you will play a musical instrument. I hope you will play something, but not to amaze me with your skill, or even less because I want to make a virtuoso of you. That doesn't come into it. What does is method and discipline. There is nothing better than music to teach you the meaning of discipline; it forces you to be exact, as if you were studying math. And it is because of that precision that there is nothing better than music to give you the possibility of expressing yourself. It is strange, and a little difficult to explain: although music has a disciplined structure, you can play with it, interpret it, and invent it. But it is all there, always in that sheet of music which you have to learn to read and which always says some things to you and not others. Of course, Francesco, this also happens in poetry and fiction. But in music you can't cheat because you can hear as the sound changes: it becomes dissonant and everyone can hear it. In the other arts you can cheat, because the limits are wider, the spaces greater. And what's more, there is also the aspect of craftsmanship which shouldn't be overlooked. A pianist or, as Glenn Gould used to say, a piano player, must have a craftsman's ability and must be able to manipulate an object that is nothing more than a very complicated and sophisticated system of levers and taut strings. But, at the same time, a pianist has to be able to read in the best way possible a work of art, an epoch, a world. A pianist has to have the skill of a craftsman, but be capable of reading a text and interpreting it. Any pianist, even an amateur—but one who has studied the instrument in a disciplined way—knows how to do this. They wouldn't be able to do it as sublimely as Glenn Gould, Arturo Benedetti Michelangeli, or Vladimir Horowitz, but they can begin to understand it from the inside. They have to overcome the same obstacles, travel the same paths, and create the same results in a similar way. And beyond this, there is talent which, at its greatest level, becomes genius. And beyond this, there is exactly that which the two characters of Thomas Bernhard's *The Loser* cannot bear.

The narrative of this novel is soon given, Francesco. Three young pianists meet in Salzburg to take a master class with the great pianist Horowitz. One is the narrator, one is called Wertheimer, and the third is Glenn Gould. The first two characters are the fruit of the author's imagination and never really existed. But the third did exist, and very much so. He was perhaps one of the greatest pianists of all time. He died at the age of fifty in 1982. The "imagined" pianists Bernhard describes are two young virtuosi who are about to become concert players and destined to make their mark all over the world. But they meet Glenn Gould and stop playing the piano because they realize they can never play as well as he can. Here, Francesco, lies the nucleus of the novel.

The problem of talent and genius is one of the most complex themes in literature and in life. It was the subject of a short drama by Alexander Pushkin called *Mozart and Salieri*. You know something about Mozart because you often ask me to play you that piece you call "Poppo-poppo," which is your way of saying "Pa-Pa-Pa-Papagena" from *The Magic Flute*. You don't know about Salieri because I have not played you any of his works. In his day, he was a very famous Italian composer at the Viennese Court; he was recognized and appreciated, and the author of operas which are still performed today, if only occasionally. He was very accomplished, but he was *not* Mozart, in the same way that Bernhard's two pianists are *not* Glenn Gould. The problem is one of coming face-to-face with genius and not looking at it from a distance, which is just about tolerable, because coming face-to-face with it is something very disturbing.

What was the story that Pushkin created? It is a wonderful myth, on which a film was even made some years ago[3]. Mozart died in 1791, at the youthful age of thirty-five, while Salieri, an older man, survived him. Mozart died while composing his *Requiem Mass* commissioned by an unknown masked gentleman. Pushkin's idea was that it was Salieri himself who, completely undone by Mozart's indisputable genius, poisoned him. But before he did so, he wished to see the composer's genius manifest itself one more time, and paid Mozart to write a *Requiem Mass* which turned out to be his very own. It is a fascinating, splendidly romantic myth and one which is absolutely without foundation, Francesco. This has to be said out of respect for historical truth. We only believe it to be true in the way that we credit Baloo with the ability to talk, sing, and dance in *The Jungle Book*.

In Bernhard's novel things proceed a little differently. The pianist who is the weakest man, the loser, is Wertheimer who ends up taking his own life, not the life of Gould who, a little earlier, suffers a stroke and dies. It is the reverse of Pushkin's short play. Perhaps even this narrative is barely credible, but the two are useful when taken together, especially when one adds a film by the French director Claude Sautet called *Un Coeur en Hiver* (A Heart in Winter). I realize it is not a book, but it is filmed like a novel; we can talk about it exactly as if it were one, as if it were "only" a narrative, a history, and not a series of images (except one that I will explain at the end). This is often done, Francesco, there is no need to worry about it, and always has been done with paintings, architecture, sculpture, and even music.

But let us return to Bernhard's novel. *Treasure Island* has the movement and rhythm of a schooner on the high seas, while *The Catcher in the Rye* has that of a large bus crossing the United States on endless interstates. And if one imagines Prufrock and company sitting in the worn velvet of an old, elegant railway carriage at the turn of the last century, then *The Loser* is a journey through a mountain path. On one side of this path is the rock face, on the other is the overhanging precipice. As if this weren't enough, it is a path buffeted by icy winds, continual thunderstorms, and the wrath of God. It was because of this that—being a thoughtful, caring, and good father—I had my doubts up to the very last minute about bringing you on such a difficult journey. But, as you already know, I then decided that I would, and for this reason: to help you understand that, in some cases, literature can damage you. There is a thin line that can't be crossed; that which would turn William Shakespeare into Hamlet, or Cervantes into Don Quixote. It can't be done. These authors could never become their characters, in the same way that you can't turn your life into an aesthetic and literary object on a stage.

I once knew a man who, since he was a child, wanted to be a writer; many people do, Francesco, and there is nothing wrong with it. But there came a point where this man's obsession to publish his novels and stories became almost grotesque. Those stories went the rounds of all the possible publishers, well known and less well known, and they always came back to their sender with the usual letters of regret. Naturally, he thought that the world of letters was plotting against him and his talent. And, of course, he thought his life made no sense unless he could publish something. So, as many people do, he paid to be published by a vanity press and out came a novel without any merit at all and of which no trace remains. In time, his mania for writing passed away and today he works as a stockbroker somewhere and I have no idea if his desk is still filled with manuscripts or not. Anyway, that novel opened with a phrase taken from *The Birth of Tragedy*, a famous work by the philosopher Friedrich Nietzsche: "For only as an *aesthetic phenomenon* is existence and the world eternally *justified*." It is a demanding phrase, Francesco, as are all Nietzsche's thoughts, phrases, and books (even his name is demanding, in its pronunciation: "Neecha"). It is the declaration of a perception of life, a way of considering existence and constructing it. Many people have fallen into the trap of wanting to live life as a work of art, and many have suffered the consequences of not succeeding. Even those lives that we consider works of art (if one can ever link the two terms together) are only so because we have come to think of them as such after their deaths. The individuals who actually lived them did not. For example, Vincent

Van Gogh was a poor and desperate man, Virginia Woolf was haunted by mental illness, and Ernest Hemingway was prone to depression, and finally shot himself, to say nothing of the existential anguish of Giacomo Leopardi, Pier Paolo Pasolini's desperate vitality, and the nihilistic snobbery of F. Scott Fitzgerald. And what can one say about Eliot, whom I've already spoken about? His first wife went mad, her life balanced on a razor's edge, and he himself took refuge in faith and religion. And Salinger, the author of *The Catcher in the Rye*? A mystery to everyone. And Robert Louis Stevenson? He took himself off to the island of Samoa from which—it later turns out—he wished he could get away.

During the Romantic era and afterward, the artist has tended to be seen only as a "genius," and the work of art was no longer sublime and appreciated for what it was, but seen merely as an extension of its creator, the "genius" who was popularly seen as being tortured and misunderstood. Thomas De Quincey wrote his *Confessions of an English Opium Eater*, and Samuel Taylor Coleridge, a great poet, Francesco, and the author of "The Rime of the Ancient Mariner," went around saying he had written the poem "Kubla Khan" under the influence of opium, which wasn't true. We know it was written over a long period and there were many revisions, but he was responding to the fashion of the day: people wanted to hear that kind of thing. Not much has changed in the popular imagination from that day to this: writing is considered to be an act of genius. A writer's life is considered to be better than an ordinary life because it is believed that an artist's expression of his or her inner self is something priceless and

beautiful. This isn't always true. Whoever has studied literature knows that the practice can be tiresome; that writing poetry has nothing to do with radiant dawns and birds chirping
sweetly in the trees; novels are hard and difficult exercises in
piecing things together, and require more of a sense of pro-
portion and measure than "genius." But no one believes this
and they end up writing bad novels like my friend, who
wanted a daring life, intellectually speaking.

I want to tell you about Thomas Bernhard because he
gives a precise picture of this modern conundrum and in a
perfect way because the three characters in his novel aren't
writers, but something more, musicians—pianists, in fact. As
a philosopher whom you will come to hear of, Arthur
Schopenhauer, said "Music is Will" (with a capital W) and it
dominates this world made only of forms, objects, and bod-
ies. Music is something more than these: it is impalpable, in-
describable, it is the soul of the world; the musician is a kind
of intermediary between this world and God, and the only
being who can perform this miracle.

And it is a miracle that Glenn Gould demonstrates one
morning to his companions on the course. With Horowitz
waiting for him, Gould comes in and sits down at the piano
and begins to play a few bars, when the second pupil
Wertheimer enters. He only has to hear those few bars to be
dumbstruck and utterly undone: "Wertheimer had entered
the first-floor room in the Mozarteum assigned to Horowitz
and had heard and seen Glenn, had stood still at the door, incapable of sitting down, had to be invited by Horowitz to sit
down, couldn't sit down as long as Glenn was playing, only

when Glenn stopped playing did Wertheimer sit down, he closed his eyes, I can still see it in every detail, I thought, couldn't utter a word. To put it sentimentally, that was the end, the end of the Wertheimerian virtuoso career."

And so it takes only a few bars to wipe out a great talent. And Bernhard adds: "Taking Horowitz's course was as deadly for me as it was for Wertheimer, for Glenn however it was a stroke of genius." In short, Glenn Gould played better than anyone else, so much better: "Once our course with Horowitz was over it was clear that Glenn was already a better piano player than Horowitz himself, and from that moment on Glenn was the most important piano virtuoso in the world for me, no matter how many piano players I heard from that moment on, none of them played like Glenn, even Rubinstein, whom I have always loved, wasn't better."

While writing these lines to you I'm actually listening to Gould, this great pianist who became a character in a novel. I want to quote some lines of music for you, even though you can't yet understand them. They are a few bars from the piece I'm listening to, the *Fugue* from the *Toccata in E Minor* by Johann Sebastian Bach, the composer to whom Gould dedicated his life. Look closely at the notes on page 123 and notice all the signs, annotations, ligatures, pauses, keys, changes. These graphic signs can create a world by themselves, like those of literature. Glenn Gould used to sing to himself as he played: if you listen closely to his recordings you will notice a voice in the background accompanying the notes. In this piece too, Gould starts to sing, following those notes which to you look mysterious, like an unknown language. Here you can learn how to recognize them and perhaps, in the future, you will also learn how to read them:

I have spoken to you of the difficulty of knowing how to distinguish in some way between what is good and what is bad, and did so using the work of Stevenson. I have spoken to you about the difficulties of growing up and of looking at the adult world through the eyes of a child, using the work of Salinger. I have also spoken to you about the difficulty of making decisions and had you spy on a man haunted by his very ordinariness, using the poetry of Eliot. Now I want to explain something else to you: the excess of critical spirit and the difficulty of reaching a point of balance. With Prufrock you have been able to ask yourself if it was right to ask if one should disturb the universe. We decided that it was right, didn't we, Francesco? I told you an old story of the city in which I was born, and of that manner of living in an understated way with no illusions, which is exactly what they do in the stifling concreteness of places like that. The question that comes now is not if one can dare, but how much can one dare. And up to what point is it legitimate to disturb the universe? What is it that we can expect from our capabilities and, perhaps, from our talents? This is why I have chosen this novel about Glenn Gould. Wertheimer, the loser, is a gray character, with no color at all. The narrator, who tells us the story, tries to understand why Wertheimer destroys himself, but he doesn't succeed, Francesco, because men like Wertheimer don't really exist: if they did, they'd be great men, and their greatness would save them. Could Salieri understand Mozart's genius? And up to what point is it that Wertheimer understands that Gould possesses absolute genius? Bernhard's narrative is purposely paradoxical. Wertheimer becomes aware of Gould's greatness from listening to a few bars of Bach's *Goldberg Variations*—a very few, Francesco. In fact, Bernhard specifies it is only "a few bars." A few bars from a piece are nothing; you need an extraordinary ear to recognize a genius from only a few bars, and perhaps you can't even do that, it is not even possible. Perhaps you need a talent equal to the person who plays them. The author states that, "Wertheimer, if he hadn't met Glenn, would have become one of our most important piano virtuosos." And we can't understand how a man of such extraordinary technical and interpretative capacity could lose out so completely. Hasn't Bernhard realized this? Is his vision superficial? Not at all, Francesco. Bernhard is trying to relate a spiritual condition in a paradoxical way (in some ways *The Loser* is a comic and grotesque novel, too): in telling the story of a person who gives in and loses, he takes the consequences of this character's defeat to the extreme by placing him next to Glenn Gould, one of this century's greatest geniuses of the piano. With Glenn Gould there is no chance, unless *the loser* is an extraordinarily talented pianist himself. Only in this case does it become a unique privilege for him (and also a kind of damnation) to plumb the depths which separate him from Gould. This is why a few bars are enough for Wertheimer, those few bars from the *Goldberg Variations*, in order for him to be stunned and have his years of study wiped away and the ghost of amateurism rear itself: "All our lives we run away from amateurishness and it always catches up with us, I thought, we want nothing with greater passion than to escape our lifelong amateurishness and it always catches up with us."

Gould turns Wertheimer into an amateur by taking away that fearlessness necessary to the virtuoso: "Wertheimer was always an anxious type, for this reason fully unsuited for a virtuoso career, especially at the piano, for which one needs above all a radically fearless nature toward everything and anything, I thought."

You will have noted, Francesco, that the narrating "I" (this is what we call the figure in a novel written in the first person) often repeats the words "I thought." After having expressed an opinion, after having asked a question, he adds "I thought," stressing the fact that these opinions and events all have to be verified, because they are only his suppositions and not universal truths at all. We only know the story of Gould and Wertheimer through the words of the third of the pianist friends, the one who is the narrating "I." Therefore, for us, this friend's narrative is the only one possible, except for one detail which is anything but small: the fact that Glenn Gould *really did exist.* He played the *Goldberg Variations,* recording them twice over a distance of many years, the first time in 1956, the second in 1982. Legend has it these were Gould's first and last recordings; and, indeed, in the novel Bernhard has Gould dying at the piano while playing the *Variations* (although it is not actually true, as he really died in Toronto General Hospital). But Bernhard has it this way because our Western culture has a continual need to recover the sense of circularity which we have lost. In the West, Francesco, we have created a narrative of history which looks forward towards infinity. The story of your ladybug is a little story which has a beginning and an end, like the story of the world that begins with *Genesis* and ends with the trumpets of the Apocalypse. Gould begins with the *Goldberg Variations* and ends with them. But even this isn't true because, although the *Variations* were Gould's first recording, his last recorded piece was Richard Strauss's *Sonata No. 5 in G Minor*. Bernhard also has it that Gould played only Steinway pianos, which isn't the case, especially in the latter years of his career when he played custom-built instruments modeled on one of his old pianos, an American Chickering of 1895. He also sends Gould on a master class course with a certain Horowitz, but never gives this teacher's Christian name, so we can never really know if this Horowitz is the famous virtuoso Vladimir Horowitz. And we do know that Gould never did take any classes with this Vladimir Horowitz.

So, except for the figure of Gould (who *is* real) many things aren't true and have nothing to do with the *real* Gould himself. But why aren't they true? Is it the fault of Bernhard or the pianist who is telling the story? And if some of the things about the real Gould are false, does this mean that the account of Wertheimer given by the narrator is also false? Is the narrator lying or does he have a poor memory? Bernhard has changed the story of one of the piano's heroes and turned it into a background event. The more Gould is a positive force, the more desperate Wertheimer becomes; the more Gould becomes a living legend, the more Wertheimer seeks to destroy himself, even auctioning off his piano, which is actually a Bösendorfer, a make that Gould detests. He has Gould arrive in Salzburg and refuse to play the one on Horowitz's course, making a scene until it is changed for a Steinway (although Bösendorfer is really one of the world's very best makes of piano), but this Gould, although little more than twenty, and still not *the* Glenn Gould he would become, can already allow himself these petulant displays.

The whole book, Francesco, is constructed around many oppositions: the strong Gould against the weak Wertheimer; Gould as indisputable genius, Wertheimer the great talent; Gould the virtuoso pianist admired the world over, Wertheimer the forgotten loser. Then Gould dies at precisely the moment when his artistic greatness is at its peak, and Wertheimer plunges into the grotesque, forbidden act of suicide. And he chooses the most cowardly method, hanging himself from a tree opposite the house of his adored sister—with whom he has a morbid relationship—and whom he accuses of having abandoned him in order to marry a wealthy Swiss industrialist. All this leads us to think that, in the end, Wertheimer isn't really a memorable character at all. But in reality all we know about him is solely through three characters: the narrator, the owner of a small hotel where he often stays, and the faithful woodsman. The latter two characters relate their story to the narrator, who relates it to us. Now don't let your head start spinning here, Francesco, it is not that complicated, and much more simple than it appears. I simply want you to understand how a simple story can gradually become more and more complicated.

You know that Wertheimer is a man who plays the piano

wonderfully well and you know it because a second person, who is also a pianist and friend of Wertheimer, tells you so. This second character, whom we call the *narrator,* goes back to the places where Wertheimer lived in his later years. He comes back for Wertheimer's funeral and tries to understand why his friend committed suicide. He decides the reason lies in Wertheimer's existential and artistic failure, which is due in part to a third character called Glenn Gould who, with the narrator and Wertheimer, had taken a master class in Salzburg. Are you following it up to here, Francesco? Good. But here there is a problem. Wertheimer never existed in real life. Nor did the narrator. But Gould did. He was born on September 25, 1932, the son of Russell Herbert Gould and Florence Greig and died on October 4, 1982. But, as we have already seen, the Glenn Gould who appears in this story shows several departures from the real Glenn Gould. What should we do, Francesco? Should we correct them? We wouldn't even dream of it, would we? No. Literature can depart from reality, and more; even "errors" like this can help us understand, and—above all—because *real* literature doesn't even entertain or cure if it makes errors of this kind. Now Bernhard has chosen to depart from reality and has it that Gould dies while playing the *Goldberg Variations,* and that he was completely devoted to Steinway pianos. He has transformed a great performer, the great genius who was Glenn Gould into a silent, unapproachable figure: he has taken away his eccentricity and put him in a glass case, turning him into an icon. But, at a certain point, something really strange happens: you feel the need to hear the *Goldberg Variations* (whether you know them or not, that is not important) played precisely by the real Glenn Gould, the one born in Toronto on September 25, 1932, not that of Bernhard. It is not enough that the narrator of the story tells you: "Wertheimer's fate was to have walked past room thirty-three in the Mozarteum at the precise moment when Glenn Gould was playing the so-called *aria* in that room." You need to hear Gould's recording because in this novel the great Canadian pianist appears as if he were silent, as if there were no music, only his actions, his words, and his presence in the background. But at each point in the book the author is telling you, "Glenn, it was Glenn who gave me the precious Steinway I had, and gave Wertheimer his Bösendorfer."

Let us make a hypothesis, Francesco. If Glenn Gould had never existed, if there'd been no second Glenn Gould who really did play the *Goldberg Variations* in a wonderful manner, would the novel be any different? It shouldn't make any difference, but in this case it does. In order to understand Wertheimer's madness, the Glenn Gould of the novel isn't enough, you do need the real one, who lies outside the novel. In order to relate a story of genius and talent like this (note the opposition, Francesco: genius and talent, not the more obvious genius and mediocrity) that is so violent, unyielding, and with no hope of escape, you need a real genius because a literary semblance isn't enough. You couldn't invent a pianist who never really existed: it wouldn't work as there would be no emotional charge. In fact, it is difficult to imagine the two other main characters as pianists, even when Bernhard tells us that they are extraordinarily talented and could have become world-famous concert pianists, better than many who are already very famous. But they couldn't have been better than Glenn Gould: that would not have been possible.

You see, Francesco, this isn't a simple story. *The Loser* is not really a story for children at all. It is dark and ends in a sensational, dramatic way. But let's go back to the story I was telling you about the smell of wood, the old piano tuner, and my own passion for the piano. You need a certain generosity of spirit to put up with not being a genius, or not having a great talent. Wertheimer only had the ambition to be a genius, while Gould *was* one. He had no need to become anything at all. When you're older you will have to learn a lesson that *The Loser* can teach you: you must have passion and generosity of spirit to love the things that you do, without trying to obtain a result whatever the cost. You've heard your father playing the *Goldberg Variations,* and for him it is an effort: his way has nothing at all to do with that of Glenn Gould. I feel lucky to be able to do such a thing like that, although I'm no virtuoso, and I want to teach you the same frame of mind.

People will tell you, Francesco, that you need a goal in order to do anything. They will say you need to target objectives and attain them, and shouldn't waste your time on activities that have no aim. They will say you can have a hobby (such a stupid word), a playful leisure time activity. You should cultivate the necessary indifference to people who pursue hobbies. It is true that you shouldn't engage in useless activities, but it is the idea of useless that is debatable. Perhaps building ships in bottles is useless, but not playing an instrument, even if you do it without any ambitions. So long as you are serious. Don't give in to the temptation of being only an amateur; you should always do things well, even when they put no bread in your mouth. But in performing them well, there is a limit that should never be exceeded: that of an excess of critical spirit, which turns people into obsessive maniacs. There is a film, Francesco, that has a story very similar to *The Loser*, but at the same time is different in one fundamental point. This is the film I mentioned before, called *Un Coeur en Hiver* (A Heart in Winter). It is not about a pianist, but a very beautiful violinist and a violin maker. I will tell you the story.

It is set in Paris. Stephane works in the family business of Maxime: together they make and restore violins. They are both cultured, refined men with a wide and detailed knowledge of music. They work with famous concert players and frequently advise them on how to obtain the best from their instruments. They are both still young men, but where Maxime is enthusiastic and helpful, Stephane is more closed, a man who thinks only of his work, you would say. Maxime has been married many years, Stephane is a bachelor. One day, at a concert, Maxime meets a brilliant young violinist, Camille (played by Emmanuelle Béart) and is completely smitten. He leaves his wife to go and live with Camille. And so Camille comes to meet Stephane and something is immediately triggered. Camille is attracted by Stephane's compe-

tence, his learning, but also by his silences, his desire to keep
his opinions to himself, no matter what the cost. Stephane
picks up on Camille's attraction, is flattered, but keeps his
distance. She is about to record Ravel's *Trio* and *Sonata for
Violin and Cello*. He shows up at rehearsals. Camille is a
young enthusiastic violinist who puts everything into her
music and even more in her own talent. Stephane studied the
violin for a long time, then abandoned it. "Why?" she asks. "I
didn't like the sound I produced," he replies. "What does music mean to you?" she asks him. "Ah, music's my dream!" he
says. But Stephane is a man dried up: he doesn't believe in
love or in friendship. Camille loves him and wants him,
but he tells her that he is not interested. She can't bear the re-
jection and, desperate, runs away from him. In the end,
Stephane finds himself tired, empty, alone, and full of regret.
He knows he is lost, he has shut the world out; he did not
become a musician because he had no faith in the sound he
produced. Music was his dream, but disillusionment got the
better of him. He did not even believe in Camille's passion
for him. You need generosity of spirit to believe in other people's love. Drying up leads you to nothing. Wertheimer isn't
generous, nor is Stephane: but Wertheimer is a madman who
can't bear himself, whereas Stephane is clear-minded in
his sterility. When his old violin teacher—who also taught
Maxime and Camille, and is the friend of all three—falls ill
and can no longer stand the pain, asking if someone will give
him an injection to help him die quickly, it is Stephane who

gives it him, not Maxime. And yet at the end of the film, he says of his old teacher: "Right up to this moment I think he was the only person I ever loved."

In his own way, Wertheimer loved Glenn Gould, and recognized his genius. When Gould dies, Wertheimer can't take it, he simply can't bear the fact that he is alive and Gould not: "Wertheimer even envied Glenn Gould his death, I said to myself, couldn't even put up with Glenn Gould's death and killed himself a short while thereafter and in truth the crucial factor for his suicide was not his sister's departure for Switzerland but the unbearableness of Glenn Gould, as I must say, suffering a fatal stroke at the height of his artistic powers."

The last pages of Bernhard's novel, Francesco, are full of pathos. Franz, the Wertheimer family's woodsman, tells the narrator about his employer's last days. He invites his old student friends over, they shut themselves up in the house for days, creating a ruckus, destroying all the furniture and antique mirrors. Wertheimer, who hasn't touched a piano for almost ten years, orders the most battered and out-of-tune grand piano from Salzburg that can be found. An Ehrbar worth nothing at all arrives. Wertheimer starts playing Bach and Handel on it almost without stopping, tormenting his guests "without exception" so that, as the woodsman says, "he, Franz, suspected since he saw that Wertheimer actually drove his guests crazy with his piano playing, that Wertheimer bribed his guests, gave them money so they would stay . . ." He pays them to listen to a piano being played "atrociously out-of-tune." After two weeks of this, he sends them away, and then—helped by the faithful woodsman—he burns all he has written since abandoning his career as a pianist: aphorisms, for the most part. In the end, he takes a train and goes to Switzerland where he takes his own life. In this grotesque, paradoxical, Grand Guignol scene lies all the unintentional comedy of Bernhard's novel. Finally, the narrator is all alone in Wertheimer's room "and put on Glenn's Goldberg Variations, which I had seen lying on Wertheimer's record player, which was still open." At the end of *Un Coeur en Hiver*, in a kind of two-part fugue, Stephane is sitting at a table in one of those Parisian cafes with huge plate glass windows looking out onto the street, when he sees Camille. He greets her then watches her walk away with the expression of a man who knows he can expect only one thing: that his hair will grow thin ("They will say: 'How his hair is growing thin'"). Stephane has none of Wertheimer's grotesque grandeur, nor any of Prufrock's clear-sighted cowardice. He is a normal man, but one who can't negotiate between what he is not and what he would like to be. He loses his taste for passion, for music, and for the flesh. When he comes to realize it, Camille is already far away.

There is one detail in all this I have left to the last, Francesco: the opening scenes of *Un Coeur en Hiver* show Stephane and Maxime in their workshop putting together the two halves of a violin. The workshop is in a mezzanine with a northern light which reminds me of the smell of wood and music that I told you about at the beginning of this chapter. There is something warm in that scene, in the way that there is something warm in the photograph of Glenn Gould that appears on the back of his records. It has the appearance of an ordinary photograph, but if you look closely at it you notice his hands, so light it seems as if they are not simply touching the keyboard, but are a part of it: a soft, naturally molded part. That photograph strikes me each time I look at it, in the same way that the slight noise of the wood strikes me as Maxime and Stephane fit the two parts of the violin together. I'm not sure why I'm telling you these things, after talking about genius and talent, and after I have said how necessary it is to be generous with yourself. You must be hard with regard to method, of course, but generous when it comes to putting yourself to the test. Perhaps I'm telling you all this because I'm inwardly convinced that the capacity to have passions, of any kind, initiates with the vague creak and smell of wood and the beauty of a printed page of music. You know very well, Francesco, that I have always allowed you to bang away on the keys of the piano; I do so not only to allow a musical spirit to develop in you (in a very simple way), but also because it is in concrete things that you can be guided by a world that is less obvious and more intense—more sensual, perhaps—a world which doesn't put ambition first.

ONE DAY IN A CASTLE, A VENERABLE OLD MAN...

I was watching you a little while ago, Francesco, while you were listening to some music. All by yourself you put on that enormous set of headphones and asked me to turn on the CD player. Sometimes it amuses me to have you repeat the names of the pieces you listen to, which is more by chance than design, because they are the pieces I have just been listening to myself the moment before you arrived. Once you put the headphones on while Alessandro Marcello's *Concerto for Oboe* was playing and—nearly right—you said, "'at obo conshert." Then you went to your mother and told her, because you know I like you to go to her and say the strangest and most unexpected things. But that time I had to explain what "'at-obo-conshert" meant. She smiled. She's used to our conversations which go like this: "Would you like some Brahms?" "No, no Barms. Mall-ey. Bob." This means that you don't want to hear Brahms, but rather Bob Marley instead. And I let you, and you fall asleep listening to "Jammin'." But also to Francesco Guccini's song "La locomotiva,[1]" Bach's *Toccata in E Minor*, Richard Strauss, and sometimes Johannes Brahms's *Concerto No. 1 for Piano and Orchestra*, when you're reassured that there is nothing to be frightened of in the great opening trill.

At other times, you go to sleep listening to a story, to those stories you already know and which we tell you exactly as you like to hear them. It doesn't matter whether it is Dumbo or Peter Pan or the nursery rhymes of Gianni Rodari[2] with the illustrations by Emanuele Luzzati. These, for the moment, are your books. There's no loser called Wertheimer, no poetry by T. S. Eliot, no Holden Caulfield, no John Silver—and thank goodness for that, it is far too soon. But one day you will find them all together in a single book.

I'm spying on you now. You are watching a Lassie film, in one of those uncomfortable positions that only you know how to find. I realize that now I no longer watch your films and pay no attention to the screen. I realize that it is you I actually watch, not the film, which I now know by heart. In that moment you are my film, a film of you watching a film. This often happens in fiction. It is called a framing device, something like Chinese boxes, when you tell the story of someone else who is also telling a story; or when a film is made about someone making a film. This is a book written by your father who is telling you stories about characters not essentially different from those you are now watching on the television.

Dear Francesco, I began this book one morning at the seaside. I am coming to the end of it on an evening when we are cocooned in the silence of the countryside, where—despite the darkness—there is a reflection in the sky that reminds us that the city of Rome isn't far away. Now you are no longer listening to the *Concerto for Oboe,* Francesco; you've gone off to bed, not without some tantrums, although generally you cause no trouble.

Earlier I said to you, what if you found those characters all together in a paper castle, that we invented, you and I? A beautiful paper castle where an old pirate, who lost a leg during a broadside, is the gardener—yes, precisely a harmless job like that—and greets all who arrive in a friendly manner, but warns them to be careful of the flowers, not to walk on the grass, and to see how quickly that hedge has grown! Old Barbecue, as his pirates nicknamed him, has turned into a different man and, it seems, a happy one. Despite his having to move with the help of a crutch, his agility is extraordinary. The paper castle is also inhabited, Francesco, by a boy called Holden who is too grown up and who capriciously keeps his surname secret. You can't believe anything Holden says, he is always making up invented stories. But he seems contented, although he has lost none of his strange way of relating things. From time to time you can see him with his wide-awake and likeable little sister, Phoebe. When Holden gets himself into trouble, little Phoebe takes a hand and sets everything to rights: she is like Peter Pan's fairy, Tinker Bell. Then there is the caretaker, a subdued man who everybody addresses as Mr. Prufrock. He has always lived by himself, and his hair is growing thin. He speaks very little, but when the days are drawing in and it soon gets dark, if he is in a melancholy mood he turns to telling stories of a far-away city where there is always fog and an old lady with a strange name who pretends she can read the ancient cards of the Tarot. In another wing of the castle lives the slightly eccentric and lonely figure of Glenn Gould. He is forever playing the pi-ano, sometimes the whole night through, but the other in-habitants of the castle understand. When the wind comes up from the south, the whole valley is filled with his Steinway and the music of Bach.

One day, a venerable old man[3] comes to the door of this castle: he has the face of a man I met in Milan many years ago in May 1985. That gentleman was eighty-six when I met him for the first and only time and his eyes, which had not seen the light for almost thirty years, seemed alive, as if looking into a world beyond this one, as if they were the eyes of a seer. He had an elongated face, the eyelid of his right eye was slightly lower than that of the left, and he wore an imperceptible smile. Yes, it was him, exactly that same man, Francesco, the one I met in Milan all those years ago. He presented himself at the door, dressed exactly as he was then. It seemed as if he were expected, and with pleasure. Our paper characters were gathered together in the courtyard, sitting on long wooden benches. There were not only the characters we have spoken of in these pages, but a great many more I haven't mentioned. I thought I recognized some of them: a young man with an English first name and a Greek surname, a Danish prince, many men at arms, and high-class ladies dressed in the fashions of their day; there were bold young men, dandies, fascinating ladies of all races, kings, queens, and princesses; adventurers, noble ecclesiasts, popes; murderers of every description, corsairs from the high seas and the four corners of the earth; prisoners and their jailers, disgraced noblemen, and whole lines of the poor in ragged clothes; and there were crowds of children. There were also the witches, elves, and gnomes you are beginning to know quite well. There was also Peter Pan, a much smaller one, much more a child than the boy you are used to seeing in Walt Disney's cartoon version.

That huge courtyard gradually became full, as if it were a book crammed with names, but in an orderly fashion; only occasionally could you hear a slight murmur. Even Glenn Gould stopped playing the second book of Bach's *The Well-Tempered Clavier*. Someone heard him brusequely shutting the lid of his Steinway and come rapidly down the stairs. A simple chair had been placed on a small stage. Accompanied by a lady with tawny hair, the venerable old man sat down cautiously, keeping his stick between his legs and resting his gnarled hands on the inlaid handle. In the courtyard there was the silence you ususally only hear in a library with thick walls and huge codices and parchment manuscripts stacked on ancient wooden shelves bending under the weight. The venerable old man began to speak in the tone of one giving a talk: his voice was delicate, sometimes hesitant, but confident. Naturally he knew down to the last detail what it was he wanted to say:

"A book, any book, is a sacred object for us; Cervantes, who perhaps did not listen to everything people said, read even 'the scraps of torn paper in the streets.' In one of Bernard Shaw's plays, the library at Alexandria is threatened by fire; someone exclaims that the memory of mankind will burn, and Caesar says: 'A shameful memory. Let it burn.'"

The silence was interrupted by a murmur, similar to a sigh of disappointment. The old man was quiet, as only he knows how to be. He moved his stick slightly, swinging it gently between his knees, keeping his face up, his chin raised, and waited for silence again. He then continued: "In my opinion the historical Caesar would approve or condemn the command that the author attributes to him, but he would not consider it, as we do, a sacrilegious joke. The reason is clear: for the ancients the written word was merely a succedaneum of the spoken word."

This time it was the old man who stopped, but it was his turn to be surprised: he was expecting a reaction, but instead all those characters were by now enthralled and dumb, as if they came from books with uncut pages. The pause was brief, then his voice struck up again with a slightly ironic intonation: "It is said that Pythagoras did not write. Gomperz ([editor of] *Griechische Denker*, 1, 3) maintains that it was because he had more faith in the virtues of spoken instruction. More forceful than the mere abstention of Pythagoras is Plato's unequivocal testimony. . . . In the *Phaedrus* he related an Egyptian fable against writing (the practice of which causes people to neglect the exercise of memory and to depend on symbols), and he said that books are like the painted figures 'that seem to be alive, but do not answer a word to the questions they are asked.' To attenuate or eliminate that difficulty, he conceived the philosophical dialogue."

It was all fluid, Francesco, as if those words and concepts had always been clear and grasped by everyone. That man knew it. He was certain everybody would exclaim: Yes, why didn't we think of it before? Even the learned citations of ancient authors seemed natural and necessary: "At the end of the fourth century the mental process began that would culminate, after many centuries, in the predominance of the written word over the spoken one, of the pen over the voice. An admirable stroke of fortune decreed that a writer was to establish the instant (and I am not exaggerating) when the vast process began."

The old man's voice became hesitant, as if his memory were asking for time to find the precise passage he was about to quote, and he said that Saint Augustine in his *Confessions* tells of Saint Ambrose and how he read by moving his eyes over the pages, seeing into their meaning, but without uttering a word, nor moving his lips. Many times, says Saint Augustine, he was seen reading silently, perhaps to save his voice, which he lost easily. The old man stopped, then added in a precise manner: "St. Augustine was a disciple of St. Ambrose, Bishop of Milan, around the year 384. Thirteen years later in Numidia he wrote his *Confessions* and that singular spectacle still troubled him: a man in a room, with a book, reading without articulating the words.

That man progressed directly from the written symbol to intuitive perception, omitting the mark of sonority; the strange art he initiated, the art of silent reading, was to lead to marvelous consequences. It would lead, many years later, to the concept of the book as an end in itself, not as a means to an end."

At this point the seats became excited, the silence broken by voices of assent: the old blind man was speaking about a miracle and he was doing it with the same delicacy that Glenn Gould showed the geometric Baroque marvel of Johann Sebastian Bach or rather, dear Francesco, perhaps *The Well-Tempered Clavier* would have been the perfect background to these words: "Superimposed on the notion of a God who speaks with men to order them to do something or to forbid them to do something is the notion of the Absolute Book, the notion of a Sacred Scripture."

Then our speaker turned to sacred books and spoke about the *Koran*: "For the Moslems the Alcorán (also called The

Book, *Al Kitab*) is not merely a work of God, like men's souls or the universe; it is one of the attributes of God like His eternity or His ire."

And then of the *Sepher Yetzirah* that says how Jehovah, the Lord of Hosts, of Israel, Omnipotent, created the universe by the means of the cardinal numbers which go from one to ten and the twenty-two letters of the alphabet, and added: "That numbers may be instruments or elements of the Creation is the dogma of Pythagoras and Iamblichus; that letters also may be used in the Creation is a clear indication of the new cult of writing."

The sun was setting in the valley and the dying rays gave the old man an even more solemn aspect. For the first time a learned man was speaking to literary characters (and not vice versa as is usually the case). They—the children of words and of the infinite possibility of combinations of the letters of the alphabet—could hear a story which concerned them and so could understand why I and so many others write books like this one, instead of occupying ourselves with the concrete, the serious and the real: because books contain instructions about how to live life by means of a fictitious world, a world made of paper—that same world that was sitting on those benches to listen to the man I heard someone refer to as *el señor*.

And the *señor* was saying: "The Christians went even further. The thought that the divinity had written a book moved them to imagine that he had written two, and that the other one was the universe. At the beginning of the seventeenth century Francis Bacon declared in his *Advancement of*

Learning that God offered us two books so that we would not fall into error. The first, the volume of the Scriptures, reveals His will; the second, the volume of the creatures, reveals His power and is the key to the former."

The talk was coming to a close, Francesco. The voice of the aged man had become a little more tired. The conclusion was drawing near. He had quoted Thomas Carlyle and before him Sir Thomas Brown, Flaubert, Mallarmé, Henry James, James Joyce, Clement of Alexandria, Léon Bloy [4], and Jesus Christ: "the greatest of oral teachers, who once wrote some words on the ground, and no man read what He had written." But he took his leave of that audience with a sentence which would strike them deeply:

"According to [Stephane] Mallarmé, the world exists for a book; according to Bloy, we are the versicles or words or letters of a magic book, and that incessant book is the only thing in the world: or, rather, it is the world."

The *señor* had finished. He had told all the characters of literature that they—made of words, letters, commas, suspension dots—were the world. At the same time, he had also said that if the world existed, it existed to justify a book. His final statements were, in reality, things he had not observed himself, but were spoken by two other men—Mallarmé and Bloy—who had perhaps in turn been influenced by others. How then to end this fable, Francesco? With Glenn Gould going back to his room and playing Bach in honor of the great old man? With Holden getting to his feet and asking one of his questions, admiring and irreverent at the same time? Or with John Silver leaning on his crutch, looking at the man with that mixture of scorn and admiration of a man who knows that, in the end, even that master surgeon, with his diplomas and Latin by the bucket, will lie hanging to dry in the sun in one of those places where, full of rum, pirates go to die, and where no one will give a second thought to all his learning. And Wertheimer? What desperate motive, what way of losing again, could he find? Perhaps too many. There is no answer to all this.

The great man rose up hesitantly, supporting himself on his stick, content now that *that* world had become *the* world. Somebody called out "Venerable Jorge . . . Venerable Jorge. . . ." He smiled, recognizing the voice, then turned his face towards him, but as ever with his eyes raised up to the heavens. "But Venerable Jorge, if we are the world, whatever meaning can the world have?" The smile on the Venerable Jorge's face grew, then almost absentmindedly, he replied: "William of Baskerville, you know very well that all the things of this world lead to a quotation or a book."

And he disappeared, as if by magic. . . .

Dear Francesco, that morning you came and brought me your book. You were still full of sleep, with your small dark eyes struggling to open, and walking awkwardly with one foot in front of the other, so that it looked as if at any moment you would topple over. You came in carrying your picture book, the spiral-bound one about a ladybug. And now we're at the end of this long letter dedicated to you. I've also told you a fable with the great Jorge Luis Borges as the main character. But there was one detail I kept secret from you: on the collar of Borges's jacket there was a red ladybug—yes, one of those like your red ladybug, the one whose story changes each time—and it had ended up there along with all the other characters of novels and other literature.

Dear Francesco, once upon a time there was a little blond boy who was playing with his father in a large park. There were a great many animals and a ladybug that flew around, which then landed on his hand. And the little boy understood, without knowing it, that the ladybug wanted a story, and he had to invent one, because the ladybug didn't have a story of its own. And the little boy began to tell a story where the ladybug was a small animal that lived hidden between the pages of books. It could cast a spell, knowing how to move the letters of the print about as it flew from one page to another, so that each time you opened a book you read a different story—not very different, only a *little* different. In the end, Francesco, stories are not very different from one another, only a little different, like the one about your ladybug, or the story of this book, which will change each time you read it—perhaps only slightly—because you will always find something new in it. Books are like that, Francesco, they have no need of the world, it is the world which has need of them. Remember the words of the Venerable Borges: *todas las cosas del mundo llevan a una cita o a un libro* (all the things of this world lead to a quotation or a book). . . .

NOTES

Anxiety

1. *Mount Analogue* by René Daumal (1952, trans., 1959). A French surrealist work, published posthumously.
2. Count St. Germain, a mysterious stranger in Alexander Pushkin's story *The Queen of Spades.*
3. Cotroneo was writing at the time of the Bosnian crisis, when Sarajevo was the center of bitter fighting.

Tenderness

1. Grazia Deledda (1875–1936), a novelist and Nobel Prize winner; Salvatore Quasimodo (1901–1968), a poet and Nobel Prize winner; Pier Paolo Pasolini (1922–1975), a poet, novelist, and film maker.
2. Pietro Aretino (1492–1556), a poet noted for his erotic as well as his courtly and religious works; Massimo Bontempelli (1878–1960), a poet and critic; Gianfranco Contini (1912–1990), a philologist and critic, and the editor of the collected works (*L'opera in versi*) of Montale (q.v.).

3. Eugenio Montale (1896–1981), a poet and Nobel Prize winner. His first collection, *Ossi di seppia* ("Cuttlefish Bones," 1925) brought him instant recognition.

Passion

1. The love lyric *A Sylvia* and the elegaic sequence *I sepolchri* are by the Italian poet and patriot Ugo Foscolo (1778–1827). *L'albatros* is one of the poems in *Les Fleurs du Mal* by the French *poète maudite* Charles Baudelaire (1821–1867).

2. Raymond Radiguet (1903–1923), an avant-garde writer who met an early death from typhoid fever.

3. Lorenzo the Magnificent (1449–1492), a member of the Florentine Medici dynasty who was an art patron and poet; Dino Campana (1885–1932), a poet noted for his instability and vagabond life.

4. Giuseppe Pelizza da Volpedo (1868–1907) painted his famous picture of Italian workers, *Il Quarto Stato* (The Fourth Estate) in 1901. It hangs in the Galleria d'Arte Moderna, Milan.

5. The review referred to is by F. L. Lucas, from *The New Statesman*, November 3, 1923, vol. XXII, pp. 116–118.

Talent

1. Monsieur Charlus is a comic character found in Marcel Proust's *The Remembrance of Things Past* (1913–27); Renzo and Lucia are the young protagonist lovers in Alessandro Manzoni's classic novel *I promessi sposi* (*The Betrothed*, 1821–23); William of Baskerville is the friar detective of

Umberto Eco's novel *Il nome della rosa* (*The Name of the Rose*, 1980).

2. Alfred Cortot (1877–1962), a French pianist and conductor; Arturo Benedetti Michelangeli (1920–1995), an Italian pianist.

3. The film *Amadeus* (1984) was actually based on Peter Shaffer's play of the same name, first performed in 1979, which in turn was based on Pushkin's short story.

One Day in a Castle, a Venerable Old Man . . .

1. Francesco Guccini's song "La locomotiva" is from his 1972 album *Radici*.

2. Gianni Rodari (1920–1980), a popular Italian children's author whose works have been translated into English.

3. The "venerable old man" is Argentinian writer Jorge Luis Borges (1899–1986), whose speech here is taken from his essay "On the Cult of Books" (see bibliography).

4. Léon Bloy (1846–1917), a French satiric author who attacked the society and religion of his day.

WORKS CITED

Beckett, Samuel. 1977. "The Vulture." *Collected Poems in English and French*. London: John Calder.

Bernhard, Thomas. 1992. *The Loser*. Translated by Jack Dawson. London: Quartet Books.

Borges, Jorge Luis. 1964. "On the Cult of Books." *Other Inquisitions 1937–1952*. Translated by Ruth L. C. Simms. Austin: University of Texas Press.

Campana, Dino. 1928. *Canti Orfici*. Florence: Vallecchi.

Eliot, T. S. 1967. *Selected Poems*. New York: Harcourt Brace.

Salinger, J. D. 1991. *The Catcher in the Rye*. Boston: Little Brown.

Stevenson, Robert Louis. 1992. *Treasure Island*. New York: Bantam Books.

ABOUT THE AUTHOR

ROBERTO COTRONEO is the Cultural Editor for *L'Espresso,* the weekly Italian magazine. Born in Alessandria, Italy, Cotroneo is the author of two novels, *Presto con Fuoco* and *Otranto.*

N. S. THOMPSON (translator) teaches English language and literature at Christ Church, Oxford. Among his publications are translations of Italian poetry, Italian prose, and the literary study *Chaucer, Boccaccio and the Debate of Love.*